WHEN THERAPY ISN'T ENOUGH

where healing can be found

WHEN THERAPY ISN'T ENOUGH

Mary Detweiler

credo
house publishers

Published in the United States by Credo House Publishers,
a division of Credo Communications LLC, Grand Rapids, Michigan
credohousepublishers.com

ISBN: 978-1-625861-11-5

Cover and interior design by Frank Gutbrod
Editing by Donna Huisjen

Printed in the United States of America

Second Edition

Dedication

To individuals carrying emotional and spiritual wounds. The words in this book, both my words and the words of others, are written to you and for you. Words are powerful. They can hurt or they can heal. They can entertain, encourage, criticize or fill any one of numerous other functions. The words in this book are meant to be healing words, helping words. They are written in the sincere hope that they will help you make sense of your experiences, encourage you, challenge you and comfort you.

Table of Contents

INTRODUCTION

"It doesn't happen all at once," said the Skin Horse. "You become. It takes a long time. That's why it doesn't happen often to people who break easily, or have sharp edges, or who have to be carefully kept. Generally, by the time you are Real, most of your hair has been loved off, and your eyes drop out and you get loose in the joints and very shabby. But these things don't matter at all, because once you are Real you can't be ugly, except to people who don't understand."[1]

I was not real for the first several decades of my life. I projected an image of myself of who I believed others wanted me to be. I did this because I believed that pleasing others and gaining their approval was the only way I could be accepted and loved. If someone disapproved of me and/ or was angry at me I equated this with them not loving me, and I was devastated. I therefore grew into an approval seeker and people pleaser par excellence!

Early in my life, long before I reached my teen years, I learned that I could please people and gain their approval by "doing." The belief inherent in this was that I needed to earn self-worth and love. The idea that I could be loved and valued just for who I was, not for what I did, was completely off my radar, totally outside my frame of reference.

The paths to earning love, acceptance, worth and value that I found, or that were laid out for me, were academic achievement and taking care of others in my family. Because of this I grew into a compulsive overachiever and compulsive caretaker. I was filled with a drivenness to always "do," accompanied by chronic feelings of inadequacy. No matter what I did, how much I did or how well I did it, it was never enough, or so I thought. The image I had in my mind of who I thought I should be compared to my picture of who I thought I was, taunted me constantly. It was the fuel that powered my dysfunctional, performance-based patterns of overachieving and compulsive caretaking, as well as the anxiety that accompanied these behaviors. I was constantly worrying about whether I had done enough, and since my picture of *enough* was totally beyond what any human being could possibly accomplish, there was no way I could ever do enough. Therefore, anxiety was my constant companion.

In addition to feeling anxious, I felt cold and alone. It seemed to me that there was an invisible wall separating me from the warmth and togetherness others appeared to enjoy. The following excerpt from Hans Christian Andersen's story *The Little Match Girl* describes my internal emotional experience throughout my childhood and adolescence:

> The flakes of snow covered her long, fair hair, which fell in beautiful curls around her neck; but

of that, of course, she never once now thought. From all the windows the candles were gleaming, and it smelt so deliciously of roast goose, for you know it was New Year's Eve; yes, of that she thought. In a corner formed by two houses, of which one advanced more than the other, she seated herself down and cowered together. Her little feet she had drawn close up to her, but she grew colder and colder, . . . In the corner, at the cold hour of dawn, sat the poor little girl, with rosy cheeks and with a smiling mouth, leaning against the wall—frozen to death on the last evening of the old year. Stiff and stark sat the child there with her matches, of which one bundle had been burnt.[2]

At some point in my childhood I either read this story or it was read to me. Either way, it resonated with me and stuck with me. Rather than dying physically, though, I died emotionally and spiritually. I was riddled with toxic shame. I was a "human doing" instead of a "human being," as John Bradshaw talks about in his book *Healing the Shame that Binds You.*

When Therapy Isn't Enough chronicles my journey to become real, come in from the cold, heal the toxic shame that was at the root of all of it, and be a "human being" rather than a "human doing." More specifically, it describes the life lessons I learned along the way. I am sharing this journey and these lessons in the hope that others will be helped along the way in their journeys to become real and/

or come in from the cold. My hope and prayer for you is that as you read the pages of this book you will not only see how toxic shame impacted my life, but you will also see how shame impacts your life. I further hope and pray that you will choose to walk the path that leads to true healing and peace. It will change your life. I know. It changed mine.

CHAPTER ONE

THE BEGINNING

One of my all-time favorite movies is *The Sound of Music.* When Maria is teaching the von Trapp children to sing, she suggests, "Let's start at the very beginning, a very good place to start." So, since this book is about my journey to become real and to come in from the cold, let's start at the beginning—i.e., why I was not real and out in the cold in the first place.

I grew up in a family in which my biological parents were together; we always had food, clothes, and shelter; we went to church and school; and had strong ties to extended family. In addition, there was no physical or sexual abuse. So why did I feel so worthless, unloved, cold, alone and disconnected from others?

This question was not answered until I was an adult. Even then, the answer did not come all at once. It came in bits and pieces gradually over time. It first began to be answered when I was a senior in high school taking a psychology course. I was fascinated by the concept that there are reasons people do what they do and feel what they feel. This course was the beginning of a lifelong desire to understand what makes people tick. It then morphed into a desire to help people live healthy lives emotionally and relationally.

I subsequently majored in psychology in college; went to graduate school, where I earned a master's degree in clinical social work; and embarked on a career as a psychotherapist. I also participated in therapy myself as a client to understand what made me tick and to hopefully make me feel better. I was unhappy, didn't know why, and didn't have the first clue how to change it.

The answers began to come soon after I finished graduate school and began my first professional job as a family therapist. The agency that I was working for sent me to a five-day training program on family therapy. Part of that training was learning about alcoholic families.

The first part of the answer

During one of the training sessions, Sharon Wegscheider's video *The Family Trap* was shown. In that video she identified and described the roles that family members assume, or are assigned, in an alcoholic family. As I sat there, I saw my family on the screen. I became so overwhelmed that I had to leave. I went to the ladies' room, cried my eyes out, and then bought her book *Another Chance: Hope and Health for the Alcoholic Family*.

Up to that point I had no idea how my father's drinking had impacted me and the entire family. It never even occurred to me that his drinking had affected me or anyone other than himself.

Over the next several months I slowly and tearfully read the book. I would read a few pages, cry and set the book down for a while. Then I would read a few more pages, cry and again set the book down for a while—on and on until I finished the book. That was the beginning of my healing. The tears were healing the pain of all the emotional isolation and loneliness. As Rick Warren stated in *The Purpose Driven Life*, "The truth will set you free, but first it may make you miserable!"[3]

As I read *Another Chance: Hope and Health for the Alcoholic Family*, the foundation of denial, upon which I had built the belief system regarding my family of origin, began to crack. As it cracked, the light of truth began to shine through those cracks. Things that I had thought of as normal and okay, if I had bothered to think about them at all, slowly began to seem not so okay. I was so used to feeling alone, empty, disconnected from others and not as good as other people that I just assumed those feelings were normal. The thought that maybe something was wrong with my family had never entered my consciousness or found its way onto my radar screen.

As I began to understand the unspoken rules my family of origin had lived by, and the structure we operated in, I slowly came to understand that I had been emotionally neglected and forced into roles the family needed me to assume in order to survive and keep functioning. Over time, these roles had become welded to my identity to the point that I could not think of myself as someone separate from the roles I was playing.

The "Hero role" described by Sharon Wegscheider fit me to a T. According to Ms. Wegscheider, the Heroes are the overachievers, the successful ones in the family, excelling in whatever area they are gifted in. I was gifted with an intelligent and inquisitive mind; therefore, I excelled in school, becoming an academic overachiever.

Ms. Wegscheider stated that what the Heroes are doing with these achievements is ". . . furnishing a source of worth for the family when all other sources have run dry."[4] She goes on to say that the high price the Hero pays for playing this role is that the goal of his achievements never is to satisfy his own needs but rather to make up for the self-worth deficit that his parents as individuals and the family as a whole are suffering . . . Yet so great is the deficit that nothing he can do is enough. And thus his ultimate goal— the one he must reach to acknowledge his own worth— remains forever beyond him.[5]

This explained why feelings of inadequacy and guilt were my constant companions; no matter what I did, or how much I achieved, my family didn't get better.

Knowing all of this, though painful, was also comforting and freeing. Once I understood this I felt less crazy, odd, weird and strange. I knew that there were reasons why I was the way I was, and that these reasons began before I was born and extended far beyond me.

Another answer

After reading and digesting *Another Chance: Hope and Health for the Alcoholic Family*, I read Michael Elkin's book *Families Under the Influence: Changing Alcoholic Patterns*. Through reading Elkin's book I realized that I not only played the Hero role in my family, I also played the role of Mother's Assistant described by Michael Elkin. In his discussion of the role of Mother's Assistant, Mr. Elkin states: "there is no question that the role must be played by someone if the family is to continue functioning."[6] He further states, "The older daughter . . . is the most likely recruit for mother's assistant."[7]

As the oldest child in the family, I had started to play the role of Hero at a young age through academic achievement. As my father's drinking escalated, he became less and less available to the family. Over time more and more responsibilities were put on my mother. As that happened, some of those responsibilities began to be delegated to me, and I gradually stepped into the role of Mother's Assistant in addition to that of Hero. As Mr. Elkin stated, there was no question that someone needed to play the role of Mother's Assistant—or Parental Child, as others called it—in order for the family to continue to function; and continue to "function" we did, in our broken and dysfunctional way.

Filling the role of Mother's Assistant/Parental Child laid the foundation for my compulsive caretaking.

What is compulsive caretaking?

Compulsive caretaking is an addiction that usually begins as a coping mechanism or adaptive behavior to deal with family dysfunction and emotional pain.

The most effective way to deal with emotional pain is to express it and have it validated by a listener. Unhealthy families, however, will most likely not permit the open expression of pain caused by family dysfunction. Not only will they refuse to allow the expression of any feelings associated with the family dysfunction, they deny the existence of the feelings and of the dysfunction itself. The individual then has no outlet for the emotional pain, so it stays locked inside in the form of internal emotional baggage.

Emotional baggage hurts, and since human beings tend to dislike pain, a need for relief from the emotional pain gradually develops and grows as the emotional baggage increases.

There are many ways to relieve emotional pain. Some people use substances. Others are unable to get that special kind of relief from alcohol and drugs. It doesn't work for everyone because not everyone has the genetic makeup for it. So it becomes necessary to find other ways to relieve emotional pain. It is important to understand that, just as we can manipulate our moods by ingesting substances from the outside, we can also manipulate our moods by becoming intoxicated with our own internal chemicals, set off by behavior. These behaviors release certain internal chemicals that satisfy our craving for relief from the pain. These behaviors then become medicators for the internal emotional pain. Some common medicating behaviors, in addition to compulsive caretaking, are:

- Workaholism
- Compulsive eating
- Compulsive controlling of eating, i.e., anorexia or bulimia
- Compulsive spending and/or gambling
- Compulsive sexual activities
- Excessive exercising

Whatever our substance and/or behavior of choice is, we begin to use our medicators with increasing frequency, increasing duration, increasing intensity and increasing variety. These increases are necessary because we develop tolerance; that is, we become accustomed to our medicators and need more to get the effect that we want. In this way individuals become addicted to, or dependent on, behaviors or substances or a combination of behaviors and substances.

Note: Individuals who are addicted to a behavior are not any better than or different from individuals who are addicted to a substance. They are simply programmed differently.

According to Margaret Fiero, "Caretaking can be more insidious than an addiction to substances such as drugs or alcohol, making it extremely difficult to identify and treat." She goes on to say that

> Lefever [Dr. Robert Lefever, a prominent addiction specialist in the UK] defines compulsive helping as "the need to be needed." There's nothing unusual about the desire to be needed, but like other addictions, caretaking is a behavior taken to an extreme. This is a perverted sort of caring that, rather than helping, turns out to be both self-destructive and harmful to others . . . Caretaking is being consumed by the need to "fix" others, to the point where you lose—or never develop—your own identity, and you smother the person you're trying to help so they have no space to work on their own problems.[8]

Behaviors associated with compulsive caretaking:

- Doing something we really don't want to do, saying yes when we want to say no.
- Doing something for someone that the person is capable of doing and should be doing for himself or herself.
- Meeting people's needs without being asked.
- Speaking for another person.
- Solving people's problems for them.
- Fixing people's feelings.
- Doing others' thinking for them.
- Suffering people's consequences for them.
- Not asking for what we want, need and desire.
- Doing more than our fair share of work.
- Consistently giving more than we receive in a particular situation.
- Putting more interest and activity into a joint effort than the other person.

I exhibited all of the above behaviors associated with compulsive caretaking and became an effective multitasker at an early age. I learned how to maintain excellent school grades while taking care of various family members. Though many adult responsibilities were delegated to me, I was given little to no direction as to how to fulfill those responsibilities. The good that came out of this is that I learned to be independent, resourceful and responsible. The bad that came out of this is that it solidified my feeling that I was alone in the world with no one to depend on. I was expected to take care of others without expecting anyone to take care of me (the essence of compulsive caretaking).

More answers

A few years after attending the family therapy training program I attended a John Bradshaw conference on shame. Of course I bought and read his book *Healing the Shame that Binds You*. As a result of attending Bradshaw's conference and reading his book, I came to see that I was an embodiment of toxic shame. Further, I learned that it had been toxic shame that had fueled the dysfunction in my family of origin. Finally, I became aware that shame is much like cholesterol.

CHAPTER TWO

MUCH LIKE CHOLESTEROL

Shame is like cholesterol in that it can be either good or bad.

Our bodies need cholesterol in order to be healthy and fully functional because cholesterol produces cell membranes and some hormones. When cholesterol is present in excess, however, it puts our bodies at risk to experience serious, debilitating, and potentially fatal conditions such as heart attacks and strokes. LDL (bad cholesterol) builds up in the walls of the arteries and forms plaque, a thick, hard deposit that can clog those arteries. This increases the risk of heart attack and stroke. HDL (good cholesterol) carries the bad cholesterol away from the arteries and takes it to the liver, where it is passed from the body. Our bodies make HDL cholesterol for our protection. High levels of HDL cholesterol reduce the risk of heart attack and stroke.

Good shame, healthy shame, is as necessary to our mental, emotional and spiritual health as good cholesterol is necessary to our physical health. Good shame is necessary in that it allows us to see ourselves as we really are—no more, no less. It enables us to develop an accurate, realistic appraisal of ourselves, both strengths and weaknesses. We need good shame/healthy shame in order to give ourselves permission to be who God created us to be. When good shame turns into bad shame/unhealthy shame, however, it puts us at risk to develop serious, debilitating and even fatal conditions. These conditions, though, are not heart attacks and strokes. They are addictions to things, people or behaviors, and/or they are negative mental attitudes such as anger, fear, depression and unforgiveness.

Unhealthy or toxic shame stops us from being who God created us to be. Bradshaw describes unhealthy, toxic shame as "the all-pervasive sense that I am flawed and defective as a human being. Toxic shame is no longer an emotion that signals our limits, it is a state of being, a core identity. Toxic shame gives us a sense of worthlessness, a sense of failing and falling short as a human being."[9]

Charles Whitfield, in his book *Healing the Child Within*, describes unhealthy, toxic shame in the following way:

Shame . . . plays a major role in stifling our Child Within. Shame is both a feeling or emotion, and an experience that happens to the total self, which is our True Self or Child Within . . . Shame feels hopeless: that no matter what we do, we cannot correct it . . . We feel isolated and lonely with our shame, as though we are the only one who has the feeling.[10]

Alan Wright, in his book *Shame Off You*, has this to say about unhealthy shame:

> Shame finds its foothold in that fault line—between what you ought to be and what you are. Unresolved, it's a chasm that invites a demonic mantra of despair: You must measure up to be worth anything, but you can't measure up, so what's the use in living? . . . Shame binds people into a prison of performance-based living. I believe shame to be the single greatest source of anxiety in the universe.[11]

Shame vs. guilt (for purpose of clarification):

Healthy shame is the source of our spirituality.

Healthy guilt is the core of our conscience.

Guilt: What I did, my actions or behavior, is wrong or bad.

Healthy Shame: I have limits. I am finite. I am human.

Unhealthy/Toxic Shame: I am what is wrong or bad.

Guilt: I made a mistake.

Unhealthy/Toxic Shame: I *am* a mistake.

How does shame develop?

Shame, whether it is healthy or unhealthy, develops as we are growing up in our families of origin. The emotional and spiritual health of our parents determines our emotional and spiritual health as children.

Erik Erikson, a psychologist of German birth, developed a theory of development that paints a clear picture of how shame, both healthy and unhealthy, develops.

Erikson's theory outlines eight sequential stages. Each stage involves a developmental task in which the individual needs to learn something and needs to make a decision about self or the world.

Erikson's stages

Erikson labeled the first stage "Trust versus Mistrust," and said that this stage takes place from birth to approximately one and a half years of age. The individual's task during this stage is to develop trust without completely eliminating the capacity for mistrust. The decision to be made is whether the world is basically a trustable place or basically not a trustable place.

The infant gets to know the world through the care he is given by primary caretaker(s). If the infant's needs are met, for the most part, on a consistent basis, the child will most probably make the decision that the world is basically a trustable place and that, though people exist who are not trustable, they are the exception rather than the rule. A child decides that the world is not a trustable place when her needs are, at best, met inconsistently or, at worst, the child is neglected or abused. A child who decides that the world is basically not a trustable place will be frustrated, guarded, withdrawn, suspicious and lacking in self-confidence.

Erikson's second stage, "Autonomy versus Shame and Doubt," takes place between the ages of approximately eighteen months and three or four years. The child's task during this stage is to achieve a degree of autonomy (independence) while minimizing shame and doubt, and to make a decision about self. The decision to be made is whether he is a capable, okay person or a deficient, not-okay person. The decision the child makes during this stage determines whether the developing shame is primarily healthy or primarily toxic.

Once the child has, hopefully, developed a belief that the world is a basically trustable place, she will begin to explore that world with a number of newly-developed abilities, such as walking, talking, feeding self, dressing self, toileting self and so on. The response the child receives from the parents for his efforts to assert independence is the critical factor in determining whether the child will develop healthy shame or toxic shame.

The determining factor

If the child's efforts are applauded, praised and encouraged (whether or not the efforts meet with success), the child will learn that it is okay to try new things, to stretch and test one's abilities, and to fail. *Mom and Dad will still love me and applaud me and praise me whether I achieve or fail.* The child learns that the parents' love is unconditional and that the parent will support her no matter what. The child will then most likely continue to work at each new skill until that skill is mastered. The result is that the child learns to see himself as capable and competent, thus laying the foundation for positive self-esteem, self-control, self-confidence and a sense of independence or autonomy.

If, on the other hand, the child's efforts are ridiculed, criticized and punished, or the parents do things for the child that the child can or should be learning to do for herself, the child will learn to doubt her abilities, will hesitate when attempting to master any new skill, and will learn to see herself as deficient, a failure, not good enough and so forth. This child will likely soon give up, assuming he cannot or should not act on his own, and will grow into a passive, dependent individual who does not develop his potential due to lack of risk-taking. The opposite extreme happens when parents give their child unrestricted freedom with no limits. This child does not develop an accurate, realistic appraisal of her own limits. This child develops into an impulsive person who jumps into tasks and situations without considering whether or not she has the necessary abilities and skills to accomplish whatever it is that needs to be accomplished.

Successful resolution of this stage, then, means that the child internalized a good balance between autonomy and shame and doubt. That child will develop a sense of independence, competence, positive self-esteem, willpower and determination (healthy shame). An unsuccessful resolution of this stage means that the child internalized too much shame and doubt. That child will develop a belief that he is somehow irreparably deficient and unlovable for who he is. This child will feel shameful about who he is and will hide his true self, resulting in a lifestyle characterized by compulsiveness and performance-based living in an effort to do whatever is necessary to earn self-worth, love and respect (toxic shame).

Three tweaks
John Bradshaw, Charles Whitfield and Alan Wright each expands and refines in his own way Erikson's theory of how toxic shame develops.

Bradshaw believes that toxic shame results from four processes occurring over time and being consistently reinforced. He outlines and discusses these processes in *Healing the Shame that Binds You*.

Bradshaw identifies these processes as:

1. Identification with shame-based models.
2. Trauma of abandonment.
3. Binding of feelings, needs and drives with shame.
4. Interconnection of memory imprints, which form collages of shame.

Let's take these one at a time:

1. Identification with shame-based models: Children learn how to be a man or woman in a marriage, a father or mother in a family, and a man or woman in the world from their parents. When children have shame-based parents, they learn shame-based behaviors. A shame-based parent is one who acts shamelessly or who manifests some type of compulsive/addictive behavior. Some shameless behaviors are perfectionism, striving for power and control, arrogance, criticism and blame, contempt, patronizing and envy. Some compulsive/addictive behaviors are drug and/or alcohol abuse or dependency, self-mutilation, overworking,

overeating or starving oneself, compulsive spending, compulsive gambling, compulsive caretaking, compulsive use of pornography or other sexual activities and abusing others (physically, sexually, emotionally and/or verbally).

2. Trauma of abandonment: In this context abandonment includes physical desertion, emotional abandonment and abuse. Physical desertion is just that—physical desertion. Emotional abandonment is when someone is physically present but emotionally absent. Abuse includes all the forms of abuse noted above. Abuse is abandonment because when a child is abused no one is there for him. What's happening is not about the child; it's about the parent.

3. Binding of feelings, needs and drives with shame: This means that whenever a child feels any feeling, any need or any drive, she immediately feels ashamed. The binding of feelings, needs and drives with shame is a gradual process that occurs slowly over time and is shaped by the reactions a child receives when he expresses feelings. (Examples: "Boys don't cry." "Girls don't get angry.")

4. Interconnection of memory imprints, which form collages of shame: When an incident occurs that causes shame we usually push it out of our conscious awareness. When we do this, however, it does not go away. It is stored in our memory bank. As we experience similar incidents and push them out of awareness, they become attached to the initial incident, forming a collage of shaming memories.

Charles Whitfield's explanation of how toxic shame develops is outlined in his book *Healing the Child Within*. Whitfield states:

> Our shame seems to come from what we do with the negative messages, negative affirmations, beliefs, and rules that we hear as we grow up. We hear these from our parents, parent figures, and other people in authority, such as teachers and clergy. These messages basically tell us that we are somehow not all right, not okay, that our feelings, our needs, our True Self, our Child Within is not acceptable . . . We hear them so often and from people on whom we are so dependent and to whom we are so vulnerable, that we believe them. And so we incorporate or internalize them into our very being. As if that were not enough, the wound is compounded by negative rules that stifle and prohibit the otherwise healthy, healing, and needed expression of our pains . . . And so

not only do we learn that we are bad, but that we are not to talk openly about any of it.[12]

Alan Wright, in his book *Shame Off You*, looks at the development of toxic shame through the eyes of faith. He states:

> If you grew up without a mother or father, you are automatically a target for shame. If you grew up with a mother or father who was there physically, but not there emotionally, you are automatically a target for shame. There is no source of shame more fundamental in the world than the broken family. To have anything less than a healthy mom and dad is to miss out on God's essential plan . . . Without a mom, I can't trust. Without a dad, I can't dream. Without a mom, I'll build walls around my heart. Without a dad, I'll never sign up for battle.[13]

In summary, whichever theory rings true for you, or whatever pieces of multiple theories hit home for you, the common thread that runs through all of them is that the images and beliefs we develop about ourselves as we are growing up grow out of the health, or lack of health, of our families and primary caretaker(s).

Truth: You can't give away what you don't have.

Jesus Christ said it this way: "A good tree produces good fruit, and a bad tree produces bad fruit. A good tree can't produce bad fruit, and a bad tree can't produce good fruit" (Matthew 7:17–18).

CHAPTER THREE

SHAME PERSONIFIED

Even though my biological parents were together and we always had food, clothes and shelter; went to church and school; had strong ties to extended family; and experienced no physical or sexual abuse, my family was still broken. It was broken because my parents were physically present but emotionally absent, thus preventing a lack of authentic emotional connection or attachment and causing toxic shame to permeate the family.

Faces of shame

Healthy shame and toxic shame each has easily identifiable characteristics for those who understand shame, are aware of how it manifests itself and know what they are looking at when they see various manifestations of it. Many people, however, don't understand shame and have no idea how shame is manifested.

Healthy shame manifests itself in three primary ways. They are embarrassment and blushing, shyness and the need for community. Toxic shame, on the other hand, has many faces. These faces are listed in the previous chapter under identification with shame-based models.

Faces of healthy shame
In regard to embarrassment and blushing, Bradshaw states:

> Blushing is the manifestation of our human limits. The ability to blush is the metaphor of our essentially limited humanity. With blushing comes the impulse to "cover one's face," "save face," or "sink into the ground." With blushing, we know we've made a mistake. Why would we have such a capacity if mistakes were not part of our essential nature? Blushing as a manifestation of the healthy feeling of shame keeps us grounded. It reminds us of our core human boundary. It is a signal for us not to get carried away with our own excellence.[14]

Shyness grows out of the healthy dose of mistrust a child hopefully develops as he passes through Erikson's first stage of psychosocial development. It grows out of the child's knowledge that not everyone in the world is trustable and that it is therefore wise to guard oneself in the presence of a stranger until a determination is made whether the stranger is trustable or not trustable.

Our need for community is our need to be in relationships with others. God never meant for any of us to travel through life alone. From the dawn of time, from the beginning of creation, God meant for us to face the world and to travel through life with others. "Then the LORD God said, 'It is not good for the man to be alone. I will make a helper who is just right for him'" (Genesis 2:18). God designed a system of interdependence. He wants us to help each other and support each other with whatever strengths, talents, gifts and abilities he has given to us.

As a child and adolescent, I was painfully shy. This was not a shyness that developed from a healthy dose of mistrust. This was a shyness born out of an intense fear that someone would find out how defective I was, a shyness that grew out of the soil of my toxic shame. My need to keep people from getting to know me greatly outweighed my need for community. The friendships that I did have were superficial. I was traveling through life alone, in spite of being surrounded by family and friends. Toxic shame was the invisible wall that separated me from others and kept me isolated.

Toxic shame

Though the outside faces of toxic shame are numerous, the inside felt-experience is the same. Bradshaw's description of this internal experience is:

> Toxic shame is the feeling of being isolated and alone in a complete sense. A shame-based person is haunted by a sense of absence and emptiness ...
> Perhaps the deepest and most devastating aspect of unhealthy shame is the rejection of the self by self. Because the exposure of self to self lies at the heart of unhealthy shame, escape from the self is

necessary. The escape from self is accomplished by creating a false self. The false self is always more or less than human. The false self may be a perfectionist or a slob. As the false self is formed, the authentic self goes into hiding. Years later the layers of defense and pretense are so intense that one loses all awareness of who one really is. It is crucial to see that the false self may be as polar opposite as a super achieving perfectionist or an addict in an alley. Both are driven to cover up their deep sense of self rupture, the hole in their soul. They may cover up in ways that look polar opposite, but each is still driven by neurotic shame.[15]

Alan Wright describes the drivenness eloquently and clearly in *Shame Off You*:

People everywhere, all over the world, chase elusive rabbits . . . We run harder when we are shamed, because we are utterly desperate for love. From the first shock of cold air in the delivery room to the last gasp of air on our deathbeds, we crave love. We instinctively yearn for it, gravitate toward it, and feel like starving people if we're deprived of it. Our need for unfettered, unconditional, lavish love is so massive we'll do almost anything to get it. The drive to attain love (and its benefits of acceptance and significance) is so great in us that we'll devote everything we have to lay hold of it. Chances are that someone has discovered he or she can get you to run if the rabbit called Love is dangled in front of your panting soul. This particular rabbit comes in a variety of shapes and sizes—approval, acceptance, affirmation, and affection. Whatever you'll run after. And if you're like most, someone found out that the easiest way to get you to run harder and be better and do more is to dangle that love in front of you . . . just out of reach. But no matter how hard you tried—no matter how good a little boy or girl you were, the affirmation you wanted so deeply was never fully given. It was withheld. So you would keep running. And you did.[16]

This explained my pattern of "rabbit chasing," (human doing), the compulsive overachieving and compulsive caretaking I engaged in to earn love, acceptance and worth. Knowing all of this, though painful, was also comforting and freeing.

Putting the pieces together

Through my training and work as a family therapist I gradually came to understand that the family I grew up in was "disengaged," as family therapists would say. Boundaries between individuals in the family were solid and rigid, with each family member emotionally separated from the others, operating in emotional isolation. The primary unwritten, nonverbal rule that kept this disengaged family structure intact was that personal or emotional things were not to be talked about.

Though we tended to have very lively, and sometimes rather loud, discussions around the dinner table, the discussions almost always revolved around politics, sports and world events. Opinions were debated. Feelings were never shared. What went on inside each of us on an emotional, human level was never acknowledged or even mentioned. The result of this was that my feelings became like foreign objects to me. I was totally unaware of them, totally cut off from them.

The secondary result was emotional disconnection from my family members and people in general (the invisible wall). I did not have the faintest clue how to connect with anyone in a real, authentic way. I functioned like an automaton, never feeling really alive.

Changing strategies

When I went to graduate school, I stopped using the strategy of academic overachievement to chase the rabbits of acceptance, value and love. As far as I was concerned this hadn't worked. I still felt anxious, isolated, empty and out in the cold. So I started to party. I discovered that when I was under the influence of alcohol and/or marijuana I felt better. I was less anxious and could interact with my peers in a more relaxed and spontaneous way. During my years in graduate school, partying was more important to me than studying. Ironically, though, I still did well. All the years of academic overachievement and multitasking contributed to that.

Back to the basics

As I moved into my career as a mental health professional, my compulsive caretaking resurfaced and went into high gear in the form of a desperate drivenness to "fix" my clients. The toxic shame led me to believe that the only way my worth and value as a therapist and as a person was measured was if my clients "got better." Further, I believed that my clients' progress in therapy was entirely on my shoulders. These two beliefs combined drove me to overwork and to take responsibility for my clients' mental health and progress in therapy. The result of this, of course, was that my clients did everything but "get better," due to my failure to give them the responsibility for their own mental health. By taking that responsibility on myself, I enabled them to stay dysfunctional. Then, of course, the more dysfunctional they stayed, the harder I worked, which meant that they stayed dysfunctional and I worked harder, on and on—a repetitive pattern, a continuous cycle.

In addition, the partying continued as I went from the world of graduate school to the world of work. Of course, it eventually led to my abuse of the substances. Not only would I drink alcohol and smoke marijuana in social situations, I'd also use them when I was alone, to medicate and numb my feelings. Marijuana was my favorite. I could count on it, depend on it to give me the same feeling every time. It was one of the few things, if not the only thing, I could depend on to make me feel better.

The "better" feeling never lasted, of course. The high would wear off, and I would be back to feeling alone, empty and broken in, what I believed, was an unfixable way. I would then get high again or overwork or overeat or get into caretaking or do something, *anything*, to make myself feel better. It was a relentless cycle. The end result of this was, of course, that I kept feeling worse and worse about myself and more and more isolated. None of it had any impact on the invisible wall of toxic shame that kept me disconnected from others.

Slowly and gradually over time, the pain of the emotional isolation and loneliness began to outweigh the fear of letting people get to know me. It was then that I began to take my first steps on the road to healing and freedom.

The first step

I began therapy as a young adult because I was unhappy, didn't know why and didn't have the first clue how to change it.

Through participation in both individual and group therapy, I was able to identify some of the wounds I had incurred growing up, wounds I had never realized I had. I was also able to identify some of the unhealthy thought patterns and behavior patterns I engaged in, gain an understanding of why I had developed these patterns and change them to healthier ones. The most valuable benefit I received from being involved in therapy, though, was that my chronic feeling of disconnection from others began to dissipate. The feeling of belonging I experienced in group therapy was the primary factor in this healing. It was my first taste of authentic, genuine connection with other people. For the first time I was with people who were willing to verbalize that they also were unhappy and confused. It was the first time I felt safe enough to reveal my real self, and the first time I experienced a taste of acceptance for who I was, not what I did.

I was simultaneously a client in therapy and a therapist. As I attempted to guide others on a journey of self-discovery, I was also discovering myself. Through the professional conferences and workshops I was attending, as well as the reading I was doing, I was gaining an ever-increasing understanding of the individual clients and families I was working with professionally. I was also deepening my understanding of myself and the family I had grown up in. The more clearly I could see myself and my family of origin, the more clearly I was able to see my clients and their families. The deeper I went inside myself, the deeper I was able to guide my clients into themselves and walk with them on their journeys. I have heard it said, and I firmly believe, that you cannot take someone somewhere you haven't been or somewhere you are not willing to go. Jesus said the same thing in his most famous sermon, the Sermon on the Mount:

> "Why worry about a speck in your friend's eye when you have a log in your own? How can you think of saying to your friend, 'Let me help you get rid of that speck in your eye,' when you can't see past the log in your own eye? Hypocrite! First get rid of the log in your own eye; then you will see well enough to deal with the speck in your friend's eye." (Matthew 7:3–5)

Another significant happening that occurred soon after I began my career was that I stopped my marijuana use and dramatically decreased the amount and frequency of my alcohol use. I was able to do this with the help of my therapist and my boyfriend at the time. For the first time I saw my hypocrisy. During the day I would work with clients who were abusing drugs and alcohol. I would then go home and get high. Once I was able and willing to clearly see and acknowledge that hypocrisy, I was no longer able to give myself permission to get high on marijuana and drink alcohol to excess.

All the years of therapy, both as a client and a therapist, slowly allowed me to reclaim my child within. Part by part, that child came alive. What psychotherapy didn't do, though, was fill the emptiness inside. Through the help of psychotherapy, I was able to change on the outside. My inside, however, was untouched.

My inside remained untouched for a very long time. Without consciously realizing it, I accepted this as normal, assuming that I had reached the end of the healing process. Many years later I found complete healing in a most unexpected place—or, rather, in an unexpected relationship.

CHAPTER FOUR

A PARALLEL TRACK

Throughout my childhood and adolescence, the emotional lessons I was learning at home were paralleled by the spiritual lessons I was learning in church (Catholic) and in school (Catholic). While I was learning at home that I had to earn my parents' love and acceptance by what I did, I was learning in church and in school that I also had to earn my way into heaven. Church and school were virtually interchangeable. We would frequently attend Mass during the school day, and religion was part of the curriculum.

I learned that my salvation was dependent on what I did (good works), not on what Christ had done for me. I learned a very complex system of checks and balances in which certain types and amounts of good works and penance made up for certain sins, and sins were divided into categories of venial and mortal. I learned that if I died with mortal sins on my soul that I had not sufficiently made up for with good works and penance, I would spend time suffering in purgatory to purge my soul of these sins. The amount of time I would spend in purgatory would depend on where I was in this check-and-balance system regarding sins and good deeds at the time of my death. This greatly increased my anxiety and contributed significantly to my sense of not being able to measure up, no matter what I did. Due to this I was afraid not only of life on earth but also of life in the hereafter.

My picture of God was of a very cold, distant, critical God who didn't care about how I felt or what I needed and who had very high expectations of me—so high it was doubtful I would ever reach them. I also learned that he wouldn't love me or welcome me home unless I achieved them. He certainly was not someone I could trust or depend on. He was someone to be afraid of and stay away from.

During my early adulthood I drifted away from church and away from God. I didn't miss anything in my life, because church to me was performing empty rituals that I didn't understand and reciting memorized responses and prayers that I also didn't understand. I didn't miss God, either. He was just one more person for whom, no matter what I did or how much I did, it would never be enough. All the years of attending Catholic school and going to Mass had not provided me with any answers as to why I felt so worthless, unloved, cold and alone and had certainly not made me feel better. As described above, the answers had come from the world of mental health, and substances made me feel better.

I went back to church when I became a mother. It was important to me that my children develop good morals, and I figured that the best way to make this happen was for them to be raised in a church. I knew I did not want them raised in the Catholic Church, though. We eventually found a Protestant church where my husband and I both felt comfortable and started attending regularly.

At first I was going for the kids, though before long I was going for myself. I began hearing things like "Christ died for me" and "God wanted a personal relationship with me." Those were totally foreign concepts to me and very difficult to wrap my mind around. What really blew my mind, though, was when I learned in a Bible study that there is no such place as purgatory. That revelation pulled a rug out from underneath me, rocking my world. It brought into question everything I had been taught growing up. I then went through a period of questioning, searching and deciding what I believed and what I didn't believe.

This questioning and searching brought me face-to-face with childhood doctrines I had been taught and had believed without question, caused a few head-on collisions with these doctrines, and brought me to some forks in the road where I needed to make decisions between old beliefs and new beliefs. The process went like this: my head would decide in favor of new beliefs, emotional turmoil would inevitably follow, and once the emotional turmoil was resolved my heart would catch up.

Two of the head-on collisions I encountered in my faith journey involved sin and grace.

Spiritual re-education

Fully grasping the seriousness of sin was very difficult for me. I just couldn't understand why Protestants were always talking about sin and putting so much more emphasis on it than Catholics did. I also had a hard time with the concept that all sin is equally grievous to God. A phrase I heard often that nearly drove me crazy was "sin is sin." I kept trying to put sin into a hierarchy of seriousness. Reading James McCarthy's book *The Gospel According to Rome* helped me immensely in understanding why this was such a difficult struggle for me. In his discussion of sin and the sacrament of penance, Mr. McCarthy asks, "What is the outcome when a sinner confesses a grievous sin to a priest and then is told that he can atone for the . . . sin by doing something as simple as saying a few Hail Marys and Our Fathers? The sinner can only conclude that sin is not very serious."[17]

This is exactly what I had concluded. McCarthy addressed this very issue and clarified my struggle by saying,

> The Lord never distinguished between sins in terms of their ultimate penalty. Jesus taught that every sin warrants eternal punishment in hell . . . Roman Catholicism, on the other hand, teaches that some sins are "light sins," minor infractions of the moral laws of God . . . Small sins, venial sins, do not bring eternal punishment . . . The Church even says that if mitigating circumstances exist, not even the gravest sin merits eternal punishment. . . . Consequently, though the Bible teaches that all sins are mortal, the Church teaches that no sin is necessarily mortal. And though the Bible never mentions venial sin, the Church teaches that every sin could potentially be venial![18]

Fully grasping the true nature of grace was equally difficult, if not more difficult, for me. Once again, James McCarthy provided me with a clear understanding of my struggle. In his discussion of salvation, McCarthy stated that "the Church distorted biblical grace beyond recognition."[19]

The essence of biblical grace is beautifully described by the apostle Paul in his letter to Titus, a pastor on the island of Crete. Paul wrote:

> When God our Savior revealed his kindness and love, he saved us, not because of the righteous things we had done, but because of his mercy. He washed away our sins, giving us a new birth and new life through the Holy Spirit. He generously poured out the Spirit upon us through Jesus Christ our Savior. Because of his grace he declared us righteous and gave us confidence that we will inherit eternal life. (Titus 3:4–7)

According to Paul, then, God's grace is characterized by kindness, love and mercy. In addition, Paul made it explicitly clear that God bestows his grace on us because of what Jesus did, not because of anything we did and not because we deserve it.

The Roman Catholic Church, on the other hand, teaches, in McCarthy's words, that

> sanctifying grace is a gift of the Holy Spirit initially given to individuals through the sacrament of baptism. It then 'abides in them,' making them continually holy and pleasing to

God . . . The Catholic is said to be in the state of grace. This is the customary or habitual state of his soul. For this reason, sanctifying grace is often called habitual grace . . . A baptized Catholic can forfeit sanctifying grace in his soul through serious, conscious, and deliberate sin. Should this happen, the sacrament of penance can restore sanctifying grace . . . Actual grace is a supernatural assistance to do good and avoid evil. Actual grace enlightens the mind and inspires the will to perform good works necessary for salvation. Unlike sanctifying grace, which has a constant influence upon the soul, actual grace is a temporary strengthening. It is the promise of God's helping hand in time of need. It is a momentary aid for a specific action, which passes with the using. Therefore, actual grace must be continually replenished. This is accomplished through the sacraments.[20]

The seven sacraments of the Catholic Church are Baptism, Penance, Eucharist, Confirmation, Matrimony, Holy Orders and Anointing of the Sick. McCarthy continued his discussion of grace with:

The Church teaches that these seven sacraments are the primary means by which God bestows sanctifying and actual grace upon the faithful . . . The sacraments are said to "contain" grace. They are not merely symbolic expressions of grace that God gives to those who believe. Rather, each sacrament is a channel of God's grace, the "instrumental cause" of grace. God is believed to confer grace upon Catholics by means of the sacraments through the proper performance of the sacramental ritual . . . The Roman Catholic Church teaches that the sacraments are necessary for salvation.[21]

The Catholic Church also teaches that an individual can earn an increase in sanctifying grace through the performance of good works. McCarthy concluded his discussion of grace by stating:

Not only did the Church obscure the meaning of grace, but it altered its very essence. Grace became the medium of exchange in the Church's merit system: Do work, earn grace. The more grace you have, the harder you work. The harder you work, the more grace you earn . . . Biblical grace cannot be dispensed like a product from a machine. Neither would the Father, having removed the barrier of sin at such a high cost, now place sacraments between Himself and His children. God wants His children dependent upon Him, not sacraments. He offers a relationship, not a ritual. Roman Catholic theology makes people dependent upon the sacraments for salvation and thereby dependent upon the Church . . . The belief that sacraments, and thereby the Roman Catholic Church itself, are necessary for salvation has no biblical support. The Scriptures say nothing about seven sacraments as the primary channels of God's grace. Neither do they speak of an institution such as the Roman Catholic Church as the administrator of the sacraments. The Bible teaches that God's grace is offered freely and directly to all who trust in Christ.[22]

Turning a corner

I eventually began to understand that the real God is not the God of my childhood. I began to believe that God loves me and cares about how I feel and what I need. I was realizing that God knows what I need and that he will take care of me and provide for me. I spent months reading Matthew 6:25–33 every day and slowly began to believe that if God takes care of the birds and the flowers he will take care of me.

> "That is why I tell you not to worry about everyday life—whether you have enough food and drink, or enough clothes to wear. Isn't life more than food, and your body more than clothing? Look at the birds. They don't plant or harvest or store food in barns, for your heavenly Father feeds them. And aren't you far more valuable to him than they are? Can all your worries add a single moment to your life?
>
> "And why worry about your clothing? Look at the lilies of the field and how they grow. They don't work or make their clothing, yet Solomon in all his glory was not dressed as beautifully as they are. And if God cares so wonderfully for wildflowers that are here today and thrown into the fire tomorrow, he will certainly care for you. Why do you have so little faith!

"So don't worry about these things, saying, 'What will we eat? What will we drink? What will we wear?' These things dominate the thoughts of unbelievers, but your heavenly Father already knows all your needs. Seek the Kingdom of God above all else, and live righteously, and he will give you everything you need." (Matthew 6:25–33)

Grasping the truth of God's love for me and understanding his desire and willingness to take care of me enabled me to begin turning my anxiety over to him. This was not an instantaneous event. It was a process. The more I trusted his love for me and his desire to take care of me, the more I was able to give him my anxiety and walk by faith rather than fear.

My anxiety, which had stayed with me throughout therapy, began to be healed. It decreased in direct proportion to the increase in my trust in God. As this process continued I began to understand that God wants to be involved in my life day-to-day, minute-by-minute—not just for an hour on Sunday morning. I was also realizing that God loves me so much that he sent his only Son, Jesus, to suffer and die for me and that Jesus would still have suffered and died even if I had been the only person on the planet! Embracing this truth moved the healing process to a much deeper level. The root of my toxic shame, my belief that I was unlovable and not worth being taken care of, began to be transformed into healthy shame when I believed that Jesus died for me!

I finally understood and believed that God wants me to have a relationship with Jesus and to follow Jesus—not a bunch of man-made rules like not eating meat on Friday. It finally sank in that there was nothing I could do to earn my way into heaven; salvation is a freely offered gift that I can choose either to accept or not to accept. I chose to accept it and began to walk with Jesus.

A critical piece

A very important and difficult part of my spiritual journey has been coming to terms with my Catholic upbringing. The Catholic Church did not lead me to God. On the contrary, the Catholic Church erected many obstacles on the path to God—roadblocks that seemed impossible to overcome.

As I read and studied, I came to see how the Catholic Church took very simple concepts and complicated them to the point that it was next to impossible to understand them. The church instilled fear and apprehension in me and solidified the toxic shame that had developed as I grew up in my family. Rather than teaching me that God loved me, the Catholic Church taught me that I was not good enough for God and would never be good enough, no matter what I did. The whole concept of having a personal relationship with a loving God was totally absent. It was nowhere on my radar screen.

As the discrepancies between Roman Catholic doctrine and Scripture became clearer and clearer to me, I became very angry at the Catholic Church. I was angry at the church for teaching me and countless others a distorted gospel—a gospel that leads to fear, anxiety and shame rather than peace, joy and love. My anger at the Catholic Church simmered under the surface for years and would flare up whenever I would attend a Catholic Mass or observe other Catholic rituals or ceremonies. As my family of origin were still practicing Catholics, all family weddings and funerals were held in Catholic churches. Each of those events became times of much internal struggle for me. At times I was able to hold my anger in check, at other times I was not able to do this.

It eventually became clear to me that I needed to make peace with the Catholic Church if I were to grow in faith and truly walk the walk. With God's help I was able to accomplish this by learning to see the cup as half full rather than half empty. I began to look with appreciation at what the church did do, rather than look with anger at what it didn't do. What the Catholic Church did do is this: teach me that God exists, that he made me, and that spiritual matters are important. The church also instilled in me a belief that church is where one develops good morals. If it were not for this last lesson, I would never have brought my children to church and would never have been led into a relationship with the real God.

I am now at a place in my faith journey where I am grateful to the Catholic Church for what it did teach me. Though anger at the church still rears its ugly head from time to time, it is quickly replaced by a deep sadness for the multitude of faithful Catholics who do not know the joy and peace of resting in the certainty of their salvation and the unconditional love of their heavenly Father. At the same time, I am extremely grateful to God for leading me away from the Catholic Church and teaching me that it is not about religion, it's about relationship.

CHAPTER FIVE

RELIGION VERSUS RELATIONSHIP

God created human beings because he wanted to adopt us into his family as his children and shower his love on us. From the beginning of time he invited the human beings he created to be in relationship with him. He never intended to give *religion* to the human race. His intention was to offer human beings a relationship with himself that was personal and intimate. Religion is about following rules. Relationship is about walking with God.

Important Note: When I speak of religion I am *not* referring to any particular denomination. Though my experience was with the Catholic religion, I am referring to "any system of rules, regulations, rituals, and routines that people use to achieve their spiritual end-goal."[23]

God's intention and desire for relationship seems evident in his interactions with the first man he created (Adam) and the first woman he created (Eve). "When the cool evening breezes were blowing, the man and his wife heard the LORD God walking about in the garden. So they hid from the LORD God among the trees. Then the LORD God called to the man, 'Where are you?'" (Genesis 3:8–9). Presumably God wanted to walk with them in the garden.

Over time the relationship was lost and religion took its place. In order to understand how and why this happened, it's important to know the history of God's relationship with the human race, as it is told in the Bible. One of the lenses through which one can read the Bible is the lens of God raising his children.

Parental love

There are many facets to parental love. Those of us who are human parents love our children by providing for their needs and protecting them from harm. Our heavenly parent does the same. If we choose to enter into relationship with him, he promises to take care of us in every way imaginable. This does not mean that God gives us everything we want. Like any good parent, God does not indulge our every whim and desire. He does, however, give us everything we need.

His promises to take care of us are scattered throughout both the Old and the New Testaments.

God's promises

God communicated numerous promises through Isaiah. Isaiah was one of many prophets whose writings are contained in the Old Testament. Prophets were people chosen by God to be his mouthpieces on earth. God would give messages to the prophets, which they in turn would deliver to the people of Israel. For example:

"I'll take the hand of those who don't know the way,
who can't see where they're going.
I'll be a personal guide to them,
directing them through unknown country.
I'll be right there to show them what roads to take,
make sure they don't fall into the ditch.
These are the things I'll be doing for them—
sticking with them, not leaving them for a
minute." (Isaiah 42:16 MSG)

"When you're in over your head, I'll be there
with you.
When you're in rough waters, you will not
go down.
When you're between a rock and a hard place,
it won't be a dead end—
Because I am GOD, your personal God,
The Holy of Israel, your Savior."
(Isaiah 43:2–3 MSG)

"For even if the mountains walk away
and the hills fall to pieces,
My love won't walk away from you,
my covenant commitment of peace won't
fall apart."
The GOD who has compassion on you says so.
(Isaiah 54:10 MSG)

God communicated one of his promises through
Moses:

"If you'll hold on to me for dear life," says GOD,
  "I'll get you out of any trouble.
I'll give you the best of care
  if you'll only get to know and trust me.
Call me and I'll answer, be at your side in bad times;
  I'll rescue you, then throw you a party.
I'll give you a long life,
  give you a long drink of salvation!"
  (Psalm 91:14–16 MSG)

Jesus summed up God's promises to take care of us in Matthew 6:25–33, recorded in the previous chapter.

Another aspect of parenting

Human parents give much to their children. We also want some things from our children. One of the main things we want is obedience, unquestioning obedience without discussion, negotiation, argument and so forth. Is there a human parent who has not used the phrase "Because I said so!" when trying to get children to do something? I doubt it. If such a parent exists, I would like to meet him or her. The same holds true for our heavenly parent. He wants his children to obey him. When his children do not obey him he, like any good parent, disciplines them.

The word *discipline* comes from the same root as *disciple*, one who is taught. The goals of discipline are not justice, power or revenge. True discipline has two purposes—education and behavior change. When we human parents discipline a child, we are attempting to teach that child self-control and respect for others, and to replace negative behavior with positive behavior. When God disciplines his children, he is attempting to teach us self-control and respect, and to replace sinful behavior with godly behavior.

From the beginning of creation, God gave much to his children, and all he asked for in return was obedience. His children, right from the beginning, had a difficult time giving this to him. Think about it: God put Adam and Eve in the garden of Paradise and told them they could have anything they wanted except the fruit of one tree. He provided them with more food than they could possibly want or eat. He only restricted them from eating the fruit of one tree. So what did they want? They wanted the fruit from that one tree. What did they do? They did what they wanted to do, not what they were told to do. Sound familiar? It certainly does to me.

God raising his children

When God discovered that Adam and Eve had disobeyed him by eating the fruit of the one tree from which he had forbidden them to eat, he did not take their disobedience lightly: "So the LORD God banished them from the Garden of Eden, and he sent Adam out to cultivate the ground from which he had been made" (Genesis 3:23).

God wants us to obey him without question, even when it seems to make no sense at all—*especially* when it seems to make no sense at all, and, as with Adam and Eve, he does not take our disobedience lightly.

After Adam and Eve left the garden the human race grew and multiplied and became very evil.

The LORD observed the extent of human wickedness on the earth, and he saw that everything they thought or imagined was consistently and totally evil. So the LORD was sorry he had ever made them and put them on the earth. It broke his heart. And the LORD said, "I will wipe this human race I have created from the face of the earth. Yes, and I will destroy every living thing—all the people, the large animals, the small animals that scurry along the ground, and even the birds of the sky. I am sorry I ever made them." But Noah found favor with the LORD. (Genesis 6:5–8)

God told Noah that he planned to destroy the evil human race with a great flood. God also told Noah that he intended to save Noah and his family from the flood. God instructed Noah to build a boat and gave him the exact specifications. God then told Noah to take his family and two of every species of bird, mammal and reptile and board the boat.

"Noah did everything as the LORD commanded him" (Genesis 7:5). God then made it rain for forty days and forty nights. Floodwaters covered the earth, killing every living thing. God then brought wind, and the wind began to reverse the flood. When the flood waters receded, "Noah, his wife, and his sons and their wives left the boat. And all of the large and small animals and birds came out of the boat, pair by pair" (Genesis 8:18–19).

Something to think about: When God told Noah to build this boat, Noah was in the middle of a desert! Can you imagine how ridiculous it must have seemed to the people around Noah that he was building a boat? Can you also imagine how much grief Noah and his family probably took because he was building this boat? Yet Noah did not let anything deter him. He did what God told him to do because he loved God and trusted him.

The human race once again grew and multiplied. God then created a people who were set apart to belong to him, to be his family. God chose Abram to be the father of his family.

> When Abram was ninety-nine years old, the LORD appeared to him and said, "I am El-Shaddai— 'God Almighty.' Serve me faithfully and live a blameless life. I will make a covenant with you, by which I will guarantee to give you countless descendants."

> At this, Abram fell face down on the ground. Then God said to him, "This is my covenant with you: I will make you the father of a multitude of nations! What's more, I am changing your name. It will no longer be Abram. Instead, you will be called Abraham, for you will be the father of many nations. I will make you extremely fruitful. Your descendants will become many nations, and kings will be among them!

> "I will confirm my covenant with you and your descendants after you, from generation to generation. This is the everlasting covenant: I will always be your God and the God of your descendants after you. And I will give the

entire land of Canaan, where you now live as a foreigner, to you and your descendants. It will be their possession forever, and I will be their God." (Genesis 17:1–8)

God also gave Abraham a vision of what would happen to his descendants long after his death. "GOD said to Abram, 'Know this: your descendants will live as outsiders in a land not theirs; they'll be enslaved and beaten down for 400 years. Then I'll punish their slave masters; your offspring will march out of there loaded with plunder'" (Genesis 15:13–14 MSG).

The land "not theirs" that Abraham's descendants would end up in was Egypt. When God was ready to bring his family, the Israelites, out of slavery in Egypt and back to Canaan, the land he had promised Abraham that he would give to his descendants, God chose Moses to lead them.

God protected his family

When the Israelites left Egypt (about 600,000 men plus all the women and children), "GOD kept watch all night, watching over the Israelites as he brought them out of Egypt" (Exodus 12:41 MSG). God never left them. He continued to keep watch over them and lead them on their journey. "God went ahead of them in a Pillar of Cloud during the day to guide them on the way, and at night in a Pillar of Fire to give them light; thus they could travel both day and night. The Pillar of Cloud by day and the Pillar of Fire by night never left the people" (Exodus 13:21–22 MSG).

When the Israelites arrived at the land of Canaan, Moses, per God's direction, sent out a small group of men to scout out the land. After 40 days they returned and gave the following report to Moses and all the Israelites:

> "We went to the land to which you sent us and, oh! It does flow with milk and honey! Just look at this fruit! The only thing is that the people who live there are fierce, their cities are huge and well-fortified. Worse yet, we saw descendants of the giant Anak. Amalekites are spread out in the Negev; Hittites, Jebusites, and Amorites hold the hill country; and the Canaanites are established on the Mediterranean Sea and along the Jordan." (Numbers 13:27–29 MSG)

One of the members of the scouting party, Caleb, urged the Israelites to move forward and take the land. The others in the scouting party, however, discouraged this, saying, "It's a land that swallows people whole. Everybody we saw was huge. . . . Alongside them we felt like grasshoppers. And they looked down on us as if we were grasshoppers" (Numbers 13:32–33 MSG). When the people of Israel heard this, the whole community erupted in weeping and wailing. They then rebelled against Moses and began planning to choose a new leader.

Caleb, along with Joshua, another member of the scouting party, stepped forward and addressed the entire community of Israel, saying:

> "The land we walked through and scouted is a very good land—very good indeed. If GOD is pleased with us, he will lead us into that land, a land that

flows, as they say, with milk and honey. And he'll give it to us. Just don't rebel against God! And don't be afraid of those people. Why, we'll have them for lunch! They have no protection and God is on our side. Don't be afraid of them!" (Numbers 14:7–9 MSG)

The people reacted to Joshua's and Caleb's statements by threatening to stone them. God then appeared to Moses and asked, "How long will these people treat me like dirt? How long refuse to trust me? And with all these signs I've done among them!" (Numbers 14:11 MSG) After a fairly long dialogue between God and Moses in which Moses interceded for the people of Israel, God instructed Moses to give the following message to the Israelites:

"Your children, the very ones that you said would be taken for plunder, I'll bring in to enjoy the land you rejected while your corpses will be rotting in the wilderness. These children of yours will live as shepherds in the wilderness for forty years . . . You scouted out the land for forty days; your punishment will be a year for each day, a forty-year sentence to serve for your sins—a long schooling in my displeasure." (Numbers 14:31–34 MSG)

Throughout the forty long, difficult years in the wilderness, Moses trusted God, and God never abandoned him. God guided him and directed him as to what to do and when to do it. Each time the people complained and rebelled and disobeyed and God became angry with them, Moses intervened for the people and God listened to him.

When they reached the promised land for the second and final time, Moses didn't actually lead the people into the land. Joshua did that. When God told Moses that he was about to die, Moses, per God's instruction, commissioned Joshua to be his successor. Moses spoke to the people of Israel, saying, "I am now 120 years old, and I am no longer able to lead you. The LORD has told me, 'You will not cross the Jordan River.' But the LORD your God himself will cross over ahead of you. He will destroy the nations living there, and you will take possession of their land. Joshua will lead you across the river, just as the LORD promised" (Deuteronomy 31:2–3).

Joshua did indeed lead the people across the Jordan River and into the promised land. When they entered the promised land, they were faced with many walled cities full of enemies. One by one the Israelites captured each of the enemy cities. Eventually the Israelites, led by Joshua, overcame their enemies and possessed the land. Then, just as Moses had done, Joshua spoke to the people of Israel before he died, communicating to them the following warning:

> "So be very careful to love the LORD your God.
>
> "But if you turn away from him and cling to the customs of the survivors of these nations remaining among you, and if you intermarry with them, then know for certain that the LORD your God will no longer drive them out of your land. Instead, they will be a snare and a trap to

you, a whip for your backs and thorny brambles in your eyes, and you will vanish from this good land the LORD your God has given you. . . .

"If you break the covenant of the LORD your God by worshiping and serving other gods, his anger will burn against you, and you will quickly vanish from the good land he has given you." (Joshua 23:11–13, 16)

A repetitive pattern

The people of Israel did not heed this warning for very long. After Joshua died they fell into a four-part cyclical pattern of (1) moving away from God and worshiping idols, (2) being conquered and enslaved by an enemy nation, (3) crying out to God for help and deliverance, and (4) God answering their call by sending a leader to bring them back to him. The people would then return to him for a while. This never lasted, though. They would eventually move away from him again, starting the cycle all over again. This cycle repeated itself over and over again for many years.

God tried for a very long time to get his people back on track by sending many leaders and many prophets to help them and to warn them. Though some of these godly leaders were able to lead the Israelites back to God, the people never stayed there for very long. They continually drifted back into doing whatever they wanted, ignoring God's rules and expectations.

The people of Israel eventually grew tired of this style of leadership and asked to have a king so they could be like the nations around them. This occurred toward the end of the life of the prophet Samuel.

> As Samuel grew old, he appointed his sons to be judges over Israel. Joel and Abijah, his oldest sons, held court in Beersheba. But they were not like their father, for they were greedy for money. They accepted bribes and perverted justice.
>
> Finally, all the elders of Israel met at Ramah to discuss the matter with Samuel. "Look," they told him, "you are now old, and your sons are not like you. Give us a king to judge us like all the other nations have."
>
> Samuel was displeased with their request and went to the LORD for guidance. "Do everything they say to you," the LORD replied, "for they are rejecting me, not you. They don't want me to be their king any longer. Ever since I brought them from Egypt they have continually abandoned me and followed other gods. And now they are giving you the same treatment. Do as they ask." (1 Samuel 8:1–9)

New leadership

The first king of Israel was Saul. David was the second. David's son, Solomon, was the third. Solomon was a man of great wisdom. His wisdom was given to him by God. Fairly early in his reign as king, "the LORD appeared to Solomon in a dream, and God said, 'What do you want? Ask, and

I will give it to you!'" (1 Kings 3:5). Solomon's response was, "Give me an understanding heart so that I can govern your people well and know the difference between right and wrong. For who by himself is able to govern this great people of yours?'" (1 Kings 3:9). God was so delighted that Solomon had asked for wisdom rather than riches and fame that he gave Solomon what he asked for (wisdom), as well as what he had not asked for (riches and fame).

No one is immune

Even though King Solomon had been given great wisdom, he drifted away from God late in his life and began to worship other gods. His disobedience did not happen overnight. It happened slowly and gradually. He began to drift away from God when he chose to love non-Hebrew women and marry them. When Solomon did this, he disobeyed one of God's commands. God had specifically instructed the people of Israel not to marry outside their faith for fear that foreign women would turn the hearts of Israelites to other gods, and that's exactly what happened to Solomon. Like Adam and Eve, Solomon chose to do what he wanted rather than what God had told him to do.

As a result, when Solomon died God split the nation of Israel into two kingdoms, the northern kingdom (Israel) and the southern kingdom (Judah). The residents of the northern kingdom continued to ignore God's commands and refused to live by his rules. God continued to try for a very long time to get them back on track. He continued sending leaders and prophets to help them and to warn them. As before, some of these godly leaders were able to lead the Israelites back to God for a time; however, the people never stayed there. They continually drifted back into doing whatever they wanted, ignoring God's rules and expectations. God finally had enough and decided that the people of the northern kingdom, his children, needed serious discipline.

God disciplines his children

The discipline God chose for his children was destruction and exile. He exiled them to Assyria. The discipline that God chose was obviously very difficult and very painful, both for him and for them. God expressed his pain through the prophet Hosea:

> "When Israel was a child, I loved him,
>   and I called my son out of Egypt.
> But the more I called to him,
>   the farther he moved from me,
> offering sacrifices to the images of Baal
>   and burning incense to idols.
> I myself taught Israel how to walk,
>   leading him along by the hand.
> But he doesn't know or even care
>   that it was I who took care of him.
> I led Israel along
>   with my ropes of kindness and love.
> I lifted the yoke from his neck,
>   and I myself stooped to feed him.

"But since my people refuse to return to me,
    they will return to Egypt
    and will be forced to serve Assyria.
War will swirl through their cities;
    their enemies will crash through their gates.
They will destroy them,
    trapping them in their own evil plans.
For my people are determined to desert me.
They call me the Most High,
    but they don't truly honor me.

"Oh, how can I give you up, Israel?
    How can I let you go?
How can I destroy you like Admah
    or demolish you like Zeboiim?
My heart is torn within me,
    and my compassion overflows.
No, I will not unleash my fierce anger.
    I will not completely destroy Israel,
for I am God and not a mere mortal.
    I am the Holy One living among you,
    and I will not come to destroy.
For someday the people will follow me.
    I, the LORD, will roar like a lion.
And when I roar, ·
    my people will return trembling from the
    west.
Like a flock of birds, they will come from Egypt.
    Trembling like doves, they will return from
    Assyria.

And I will bring them home again,"
    says the Lord.

Israel surrounds me with lies and deceit,
    but Judah still obeys God
    and is faithful to the Holy One.
(Hosea 11:1–12)

The people of Judah, however, didn't stay faithful to the Holy One for very long. They also fell into doing their own thing and ignoring God's commands. Approximately 200 years after he had exiled the northern kingdom to Assyria, God exiled the southern kingdom (Judah) to Babylon.

This is what the Lord says:

"The people of Judah have sinned again and again,
    and I will not let them go unpunished!
They have rejected the instruction of the Lord,
    refusing to obey his decrees.
They have been led astray by the same lies
    that deceived their ancestors.
So I will send down fire on Judah,
    and all the fortresses of Jerusalem will be
destroyed." (Amos 2:4–5)

When God destroyed the fortresses of Jerusalem, the temple was also destroyed. The city lay in ruins.

Important Point: Though God sent his people into exile, he did not abandon them. He continually sent messages of encouragement and hope to them, as well as promises of restoration, through the prophets Ezekiel, Isaiah and Jeremiah. Some of these messages and promises are:

"Therefore, tell the exiles, 'This is what the Sovereign LORD says: Although I have scattered you in the countries of the world, I will be a sanctuary to you during your time of exile.'" (Ezekiel 11:16)

"Do not be afraid, for I am with you.
    I will gather you and your children from east and west.
I will say to the north and south,
        'Bring my sons and daughters back to Israel
        from the distant corners of the earth.
Bring all who claim me as their God,
        for I have made them for my glory.
        It was I who created them.'" (Isaiah 43:5–7)

"So do not be afraid, Jacob, my servant;
        do not be dismayed, Israel,"
        says the LORD.
"For I will bring you home again from distant lands,
        and your children will return from their exile.
Israel will return to a life of peace and quiet,
        and no one will terrorize them.
For I am with you and will save you,"
        says the LORD.
"I will completely destroy the nations where
        I have scattered you,
        but I will not completely destroy you.

I will discipline you, but with justice;
    I cannot let you go unpunished."
(Jeremiah 30:10–11)

"Nevertheless, the time will come when I will heal Jerusalem's wounds and give it prosperity and true peace. I will restore the fortunes of Judah and Israel and rebuild their towns. I will cleanse them of their sins against me and forgive all their sins of rebellion. Then this city will bring me joy, glory, and honor before all the nations of the earth! The people of the world will see all the good I do for my people, and they will tremble with awe at the peace and prosperity I provide for them." (Jeremiah 33:6–9)

"Give them this message from the Sovereign LORD: I will gather the people of Israel from among the nations. I will bring them home to their own land from the places where they have been scattered. I will unify them into one nation on the mountains of Israel. One king will rule them all; no longer will they be divided into two nations or into two kingdoms." (Ezekiel 37:21–22)

God eventually made good on his promises, as he always does, and brought to an end the disciplining process of the peoples of Israel and of Judah. Though he facilitated their return to their homeland, many Jews chose not to return. They remained scattered throughout the known world. The Jews who did return, particularly the leaders, were determined to start over by not repeating the mistakes and sins of their past. The experience of having lived through war, destruction, captivity and exile led many of them to embrace radical obedience as a major component of their faith. "The idea that right living would bring divine approval became an obsession among some religious people. . . . Their experience fortified their belief that the righteous will prosper but the wicked will perish."[24]

Could it be that this is where, when and why relationship began to die and religion began to be born?

Reason for the rules

The people of Israel and the people of Judah who returned to their homeland from exile had good intentions—they wanted to obey God. The mistake they made was that their desire to obey God was rooted in fear, not love. They were afraid of what God would do to them if they didn't obey him. This is totally understandable in light of what they had been through—war, destruction, captivity and exile. The problem with this is that God wants us to obey him because we love him and trust him, not because we're afraid of him.

Important Note: I realize that there are many verses in the Bible that tell us to fear the Lord, such as Proverbs 9:10: "Fear of the LORD is the foundation of wisdom." The fear that Solomon is referring to in the book of Proverbs is not fear as in being afraid that we'll be hurt or scared of a harsh punishment. It is more like awe or respect. God himself spoke of this kind of fear through the prophet Jeremiah: "Have you no respect for me? Why don't you tremble in my presence?" (Jeremiah 5:22). The writer of the book of Acts also spoke of this kind of fear when he said: "The story of what happened spread quickly all through Ephesus, to Jews and Greeks alike. A solemn fear descended on the city, and the name of the Lord Jesus was greatly honored" (Acts 19:17).

Those of us who are human parents give our children rules to live by because we love them. The rules provide needed boundaries, protecting and guiding them. In turn, we want our children to follow our rules because they love us and value the relationship they have with us, not because they are afraid of us. The same is true of our heavenly parent. When God gave the Israelites, his chosen people, his family, rules to live by, he was taking care of them, protecting them. He never meant for the rules to replace the relationship he had with them. He meant for the rules to highlight that relationship. He wanted the Israelites to be set apart from the nations surrounding them. He wanted them to live by a higher standard than their neighbors and to be identified to other nations as his people, his family.

Somewhere along the line the Israelites got the idea that they only had to follow God's rules to be acceptable to him and to become part of his family. They forgot that though he had sent them into exile, he had not ejected them from his family. He continued to be their Father. He was merely disciplining them for their misbehavior.

Important Point: God did not want the Israelites to follow his rules so that they could become his children. They *already were* his children. God wanted them to follow his rules so that the world would *know* that they were his children.

When the Israelites started misunderstanding the purpose of God's laws, and then started acting on the basis of that misunderstanding, religion was born. As a result of this misunderstanding, the Israelites shifted their focus from their relationship with God to the rules God had given them, putting their trust in the rules and in their own ability to follow them rather than putting their trust in God. Their view of God as a loving parent who would take care of them was replaced by a view of God as an angry parent who would punish them if they disobeyed him. Again, this is understandable in light of their experience of having been sent into exile. They moved from being dependent on God to being dependent on themselves. This is the very essence of religion.

CHAPTER SIX

THEN JESUS CAME

Jesus came to earth to restore what had been lost, a personal relationship with God. Jesus is God's ultimate gift to humanity. My own personal relationship with God through Jesus is the unexpected relationship in which I found complete healing for my emotional and spiritual wounds. I celebrate my relationship with Jesus every year at Christmas.

Having a personal relationship with God through Christ—i.e., walking with Jesus in my daily life—was all new to me, and, as I read and studied and lived it, I began to realize that the newness I was experiencing was not unlike the newness the people of Jesus' day experienced when they met him in the flesh. Beginning right away when he was born, the experience of those who met him convinced them that he was something new, something different, something out of the ordinary.

> That night there were shepherds staying in the fields nearby, guarding their flocks of sheep. Suddenly, an angel of the Lord appeared among them, and the radiance of the Lord's glory

surrounded them. They were terrified, but the angel reassured them. "Don't be afraid!' he said. "I bring you good news that will bring great joy to all people. The Savior—yes, the Messiah, the Lord—has been born today in Bethlehem, the city of David! And you will recognize him by this sign: You will find a baby wrapped snugly in strips of cloth, lying in a manger."

Suddenly, the angel was joined by a vast host of others—the armies of heaven—praising God and saying,

> "Glory to God in highest heaven,
> and peace on earth to those with whom God is pleased."

When the angels had returned to heaven, the shepherds said to each other, "Let's go to Bethlehem! Let's see this thing that has happened, which the Lord has told us about."

They hurried to the village and found Mary and Joseph. And there was the baby, lying in the manger. After seeing him, the shepherds told everyone what had happened and what the angel had said to them about this child. All who heard the shepherds' story were astonished, but Mary kept all these things in her heart and thought about them often (Luke 2:8–19)

Other than the accounts of the events surrounding his birth in Bethlehem, we know very little about Jesus' childhood, except that he grew up in Nazareth. The Gospel of Luke tells us that "there the child grew up healthy and strong. He was filled with wisdom, and God's favor was on him" (Luke 2:40). As such, it is hard to believe that he would not have stood out in his village as someone who was somehow different, not ordinary.

The only scriptural account we have of Jesus' childhood describes an incident that occurred when he was 12 years old:

> Every year Jesus' parents traveled to Jerusalem for the Feast of Passover. When he was twelve years old, they went up as they always did for the Feast. When it was over and they left for home, the child Jesus stayed behind in Jerusalem, but his parents didn't know it. Thinking he was somewhere in the company of pilgrims, they journeyed for a whole day and then began looking for him among relatives and neighbors. When they didn't find him, they went back to Jerusalem looking for him.
>
> The next day they found him in the Temple seated among the teachers, listening to them and asking questions. The teachers were all quite taken with him, impressed with the sharpness of his answers. But his parents were not impressed; they were upset and hurt.
>
> His mother said, "Young man, why have you done this to us? Your father and I have been half out of our minds looking for you."

He said, "Why were you looking for me? Didn't you know that I had to be here, dealing with the things of my Father?" (Luke 2:41–49 MSG)

Following this exchange, "he returned to Nazareth with them and was obedient to them" (Luke 2:51). We are then told that following this incident "Jesus grew in wisdom and in stature and in favor with God and all the people" (Luke 2:52). Again, it is hard to believe that, in that light, people would not have recognized that Jesus was not an ordinary child.

The pattern continues

When Jesus began his earthly ministry at the age of 30, everything he said and everything he did, not surprisingly, was marked by being something new, something different, something extraordinary. He healed the sick, the lame, the blind, the deaf and those possessed by demons. At one point we are told that "as the sun went down that evening, people throughout the village brought sick family members to Jesus. No matter what their diseases were, the touch of his hand healed every one" (Luke 4:40). He also raised people from the dead and fed thousands of people with only a few loaves of bread and a few fish.

His teachings were also filled with concepts that were new and different. Early in his ministry Jesus spelled out God's expectations for every conceivable part of our lives in his most famous sermon, the Sermon on the Mount. (See Appendix One.) As you read and ponder these expectations and consider the lifestyle Jesus modeled and calls us to live, it becomes clear that God's standards in no way, shape or form match the world's standards. As a matter of fact, God's standards and expectations contradict and challenge the commonly accepted values and standards of the world. They turn the world's standards upside down and inside out. The world says to take revenge on those who do us wrong; Jesus said to forgive them and be kind to them. The world says to hate our enemies; Jesus said to love them and pray for them. The world says to let people know the good things we've done so they will admire us; Jesus said to keep those good things secret. The world says to accumulate as much wealth and possessions as possible and hold onto them; Jesus said to give them away.

Toward the end of the Sermon on the Mount, Jesus acknowledged that the lifestyle he was asking people to live is difficult. "You can enter God's Kingdom only through the narrow gate. The highway to hell is broad, and its gate is wide for the many who choose that way. But the gateway to life is very narrow and the road is difficult, and only a few ever find it" (Matthew 7:13–14).

One of the most controversial concepts Jesus taught was that loving people is more important than obeying the law. The Jewish law at that time consisted of the Ten Commandments God gave Moses on Mount Sinai, and more than 2,000 laws Jewish religious leaders had developed to help people keep the Ten Commandments (See Appendix Two). One way Jesus modeled this teaching was by deliberately disobeying, and thereby challenging, their law that no work was to be done on the Sabbath.

At about that time Jesus was walking through some grainfields on the Sabbath. His disciples were hungry, so they began breaking off some heads of grain and eating them. But some Pharisees saw them do it and protested, "Look, your disciples are breaking the law by harvesting grain on the Sabbath."

Jesus said to them, . . . "You would not have condemned my innocent disciples if you knew the meaning of this Scripture: 'I want you to show mercy, not offer sacrifices.' For the Son of Man is Lord, even over the Sabbath!" (Matthew 12:1–3, 7–8)

The most important teaching

The most important and most controversial of his teachings was that following the rules will not get one to heaven. After all, this was central to his whole purpose for coming to earth in human form. He continually told people that the way to God and to eternal life was not religion (i.e., obeying the law); it was relationship (believing that he is who he said he is, the Son of God, and following him). He continually pointed to himself as the way to heaven.

When speaking with his disciple Nathanael, "he said, 'I tell you the truth, you will all see heaven open and the angels of God going up and down on the Son of Man, the one who is the stairway between heaven and earth'" (John 1:51).

When talking to Martha, Lazarus's sister, Jesus said: "'I am the resurrection and the life. Anyone who believes in me will live, even after dying. Everyone who lives in me and believes in me will never ever die'" (John 11:25–26).

When speaking to the religious leaders Jesus said: "'You search the Scriptures because you think they give you eternal life. But the Scriptures point to me! Yet you refuse to come to me to receive this life'" (John 5:39–40).

Five days before his death Jesus said the following words to a crowd in Jerusalem: "'If you trust me, you are trusting not only me, but also God who sent me. For when you see me, you are seeing the one who sent me. I have come as a light to shine in this dark world, so that all who put their trust in me will no longer remain in the dark" (John 12:44–46).

At the last meal Jesus shared with the apostles before his death he again made the point that trusting in him, not in a set of rules or laws, is the way to God. He said: "'Don't let your hearts be troubled. Trust in God, and trust also in me. . . . I am the way, the truth, and the life. No one can come to the Father except through me" (John 14:1, 6).

Reactions to Jesus

Many people believed in Jesus and thronged to him. "Large crowds soon surrounded Jesus, and he couldn't publicly enter a town anywhere. He had to stay out in the secluded places, but people from everywhere kept coming to him" (Mark 1:45). "News about him spread as far as Syria, and people soon began bringing to him all who were sick. And whatever their sickness or disease, or if they were demon possessed or epileptic or paralyzed— he healed them all. Large crowds followed him wherever he went" (Matthew 4:24–25).

These people knew who Jesus was and where his power came from. "As the boy came forward, the demon knocked him to the ground and threw him into a violent convulsion. But Jesus rebuked the evil spirit and healed the boy. Then he gave him back to his father. Awe gripped the people as they saw this majestic display of God's power" (Luke 9:42–43).

The religious leaders, however, refused to believe in Jesus in spite of the evidence their own eyes and ears were giving them. (See Appendix Three.)

They were outraged at Jesus for his constant challenging of their core beliefs, and there is no indication in Scripture that they considered changing their beliefs:

> Then Jesus went over to their synagogue, where he noticed a man with a deformed hand. The Pharisees asked Jesus, "Does the law permit a person to work by healing on the Sabbath?" (They were hoping he would say yes, so they could bring charges against him.)
>
> And he answered, "If you had a sheep that fell into a well on the Sabbath, wouldn't you work to pull it out? Of course you would. And how much more valuable is a person than a sheep! Yes, the law permits a person to do good on the Sabbath."
>
> Then he said to the man, "Hold out your hand." So the man held out his hand, and it was restored, just like the other one! Then the Pharisees called a meeting to plot how to kill Jesus. (Matthew 12:9–14)

All about love

Jesus' entire earthly ministry was characterized by love. He preached it and lived it.

His final act of love for humanity, while in his earthly body, was allowing himself to be crucified. He understood that the ultimate purpose for which he had come to earth was to offer himself as a sacrifice for all the sins and wrongdoings of all humankind, thus giving the children of God the opportunity to transition from the old covenant to the new covenant, from religion to relationship. Throughout the three years of his earthly ministry he never lost sight of that purpose. As he went about ministering to people by teaching them and healing them, he was always moving toward the fulfillment of his ultimate purpose. "Jesus went through the towns and villages, teaching as he went, always pressing on toward Jerusalem" (Luke 13:22).

If you want a picture of pure, perfect love, picture Jesus, bloody and beaten beyond recognition and hanging on a wooden cross. He did not have to stay hanging there. He *chose* to stay hanging there. It was not nails that held him to that cross. It was love, love for each and every one of us, past, present and future, including the people who had crucified him and those who mocked and abused him as he hung on the cross.

> The people passing by shouted abuse, shaking their heads in mockery. "Look at you now!" they yelled at him. "You said you were going to destroy the Temple and rebuild it in three days. Well then, if you are the Son of God, save yourself and come down from that cross!"

The leading priests, the teachers of religious law, and the elders also mocked Jesus. "He saved others," they scoffed, "but he can't save himself! So he is the King of Israel, is he? Let him come down from that cross right now, and we will believe in him! He trusted God, so let God rescue him now if he wants him! For he said, 'I am the Son of God.'" (Matthew 27:39–43)

What the priests, teachers of religious law, and elders didn't understand was that Jesus stayed on that cross because he loved them. If Jesus had come down from that cross, which he was more than capable of doing, he would not have given the human race the opportunity to transition from the old covenant to the new covenant, from religion to relationship. He would not have become "the stairway between heaven and earth."

The covenants

The concept of God creating a new covenant that would accomplish for his people what the old covenant had failed to accomplish was prophesied by Jeremiah:

"The day is coming," says the LORD, "when I will make a new covenant with the people of Israel and Judah. This covenant will not be like the one I made with their ancestors when I took them by the hand and brought them out of the land of Egypt. They broke that covenant, though I loved them as a husband loves his wife," says the LORD.

"But this is the new covenant I will make with the people of Israel after those days," says the LORD. "I will put my instructions deep within them, and I will write them on their hearts. I will be their God, and they will be my people. And they will not need to teach their neighbors, nor will they need to teach their relatives, saying, 'You should know the LORD.' For everyone, from the least to the greatest, will know me already," says the LORD. "And I will forgive their wickedness, and I will never again remember their sins." (Jeremiah 31:31–34)

The writer of the book of Hebrews in the New Testament stated, "If the first covenant had been faultless, there would have been no need for a second covenant to replace it" (Hebrews 8:7).

John Fischer, in his book *12 Steps for the Recovering Pharisee (Like Me)*, explains this quite clearly:

The Old Covenant requires a standard of performance and a reason to be obedient to it. But the standard, in its truest form, is impossible to pull off consistently. It could be argued that this is the whole point of God's dealings with humanity through the covenants. The Old Covenant is there to break us, to show us that we cannot live according to its precepts—that sin and selfishness dwell in us to a significant degree so as to rule out the possibility of following even the clear call of

Jesus to love God, self, and others. This inability to follow the standard, along with its accompanying humility, qualifies us for a Savior—someone who will fulfill the law on our behalf and grant us righteousness as a free gift. This is God's grace as given to us in the New Covenant through the death and resurrection of our Lord and Savior Jesus Christ.[25]

The apostle Paul also explained this quite clearly and eloquently in his letter to the church in Rome. (See Appendix Four.)

Why did Jesus have to die on a cross?

In order to understand why Jesus had to die on a cross—i.e., shed his blood—to effect the transition from the old covenant to the new covenant, we need to go back to when the Israelites were set free from slavery in Egypt.

Two months after they left Egypt, the Israelites arrived in the wilderness of Sinai and set up camp at the base of Mount Sinai. While there, Moses had a personal encounter with God. During that encounter God told Moses "'I will come to you in a thick cloud, Moses, so the people themselves can hear me when I speak with you. Then they will always trust you'" (Exodus 19:9). As always, God made good on his promise:

> On the morning of the third day, thunder roared and lightning flashed, and a dense cloud came down on the mountain. There was a long, loud

blast from a ram's horn, and all the people trembled. Moses led them out from the camp to meet with God, and they stood at the foot of the mountain. All of Mount Sinai was covered with smoke because the LORD had descended on it in the form of fire. The smoke billowed into the sky like smoke from a brick kiln, and the whole mountain shook violently. As the blast of the ram's horn grew louder and louder, Moses spoke, and God thundered his reply. The LORD came down on the top of Mount Sinai and called Moses to the top of the mountain. So Moses climbed the mountain. (Exodus 19:16–20)

Moses subsequently went up and down the mountain several times. During the times Moses was on the mountain God told him how he wanted the Israelites to behave. Moses would then come down from the mountain and explain God's expectations to the people. Then one day God said to Moses, "Have the people of Israel build me a holy sanctuary so I can live among them. You must build this Tabernacle and its furnishings exactly according to the pattern I will show you" (Exodus 25:8–9). God then proceeded to give Moses explicit directions down to the last detail as to how to build every inch of the tabernacle and every one of its furnishings and contents. He also gave Moses detailed instructions as to how the people were to worship him in the tabernacle.

One of the furnishings for the tabernacle was an altar upon which animals would be sacrificed as an offering to atone for sin. One of God's instructions regarding this altar was, "Make horns for each of its four corners so that the horns and altar are all one piece" (Exodus 27:2). When the altar was finished, God told Moses, "Place the altar of burnt offering in front of the Tabernacle entrance" (Exodus 40:6).

God appointed Moses' brother Aaron and Aaron's sons to serve as his priests. God told Moses how and when to anoint and ordain Aaron and his sons, consecrating them to perform their priestly duties. One of these duties was the performance of the ritual in which animals were burned for the sin offering. Sin was considered to be "anything that violates one of the Lord's commands" (Leviticus 4:2). Once a person or persons sinned, the burnt offering was necessary in order to cleanse that person or persons of their sin and make them right with God.

The ritual of the burnt offering, as instructed by God to Moses, was as follows:

> "They must lay a hand on the head of the sin offering and slaughter it at the place where burnt offerings are slaughtered. Then the priest will dip his finger in the blood and put it on the horns of the altar for burnt offerings. He will pour out the rest of the blood at the base of the altar. Then he must remove all the goat's fat, just as he does with the fat of the peace offering. He will burn the fat on the altar, and it will be a pleasing aroma to the Lord. Through this process, the priest will purify the people, making them right with the Lord, and they will be forgiven." (Leviticus 4:29–31)

During one of the conversations between God and Moses, God explained to Moses why the killing of animals was necessary to atone for sin: "For the life of the body is in its blood. I have given you the blood on the altar to purify you, making you right with the LORD. It is the blood, given in exchange for a life, that makes purification possible" (Leviticus 17:11).

The sacrificing of animals needed to be continually repeated because these blood sacrifices, or burnt offerings, atoned for sin partially and for a short time. When Christ shed his blood on the cross, however, it was a once for all time sacrifice, making future sacrifices unnecessary. He was the Lamb of God, the perfect sacrifice God provided that would make all future sacrifices unnecessary. The blood of bulls and goats and lambs was no longer needed to cleanse people from their sin. Jesus' blood covers all who accept his free gift of salvation, forgiving all their sins—past, present and future—for all time.

The definitive sign that Jesus had completed the work he had come to earth to do—i.e., restore the relationship that had been lost between God and humanity and thereby establish the new covenant—was that at the moment of his death the veil in the temple in Jerusalem ripped in half. "And Jesus cried out with a loud voice, and breathed His last. Then the veil of the temple was torn in two, from top to bottom" (Mark 15:37–38 NKJV).

CHAPTER SEVEN

THE VEIL

The significance of the veil in the temple tearing at the moment of Jesus' death is lost on many 21st-century churchgoers. To 1st-century Jews who believed that Jesus was the messiah, however, the significance was enormous. The tearing of the veil meant that individuals now had direct access to God. They no longer needed a priest to act as an intermediary, representing them before God.

Background

When God began to instruct Moses how to build the temple's furnishings and contents, the first set of plans he gave Moses were for an ark. "Have the people make an Ark of acacia wood—a sacred chest 45 inches long, 27 inches wide, and 27 inches high.... When the Ark is finished, place inside it the stone tablets inscribed with the terms of the covenant, which I will give you" (Exodus 25:10, 16).

God then told Moses,

> "You shall make a veil woven of blue, purple and scarlet thread, and fine woven linen. It shall be woven with an artistic design of cherubim. You

shall hang it upon the four pillars of acacia wood overlaid with gold. Their hooks shall be gold, upon four sockets of silver. And you shall hang the veil from the clasps. Then you shall bring the ark of the Testimony in there, behind the veil. The veil shall be a divider for you between the holy place and the Most Holy." (Exodus 26:31–33 NKJV)

"When the LORD finished speaking with Moses on Mount Sinai, he gave him the two stone tablets inscribed with the terms of the covenant, written by the finger of God" (Exodus 31:18). When Moses came down from the mountain he carried with him the two stone tablets. When he arrived at the Israelite camp he found that the people had turned away from God in his absence and built a gold calf to worship as their god. They were dancing in celebration at the altar of the gold calf as Moses entered the camp. "Moses saw the calf and the dancing, and he burned with anger. He threw the stone tablets to the ground, smashing them at the foot of the mountain" (Exodus 32:19). He then interceded with God for the people, as God was very angry at the Israelites for their idolatry. Due to God's willingness to listen to Moses and Moses' willingness to advocate for the people, God did not punish them as severely as he may have initially intended to.

Sometime later "the LORD told Moses, 'Chisel out two stone tablets like the first ones. I will write on them the same words that were on the tablets you smashed. Be ready in the morning to climb up Mount Sinai and present yourself to me on the top of the mountain'" (Exodus 34:1–2). Moses went back up on the mountain as God commanded and returned to the Israelite camp with two new stone tablets inscribed with the Ten Commandments.

The Israelites then began to build the tabernacle and its furnishings. When the tabernacle and all its contents were completed, Moses set up the tabernacle according to God's instructions. He hung the veil between the Holy Place and the Most Holy Place; he put the two stone tablets inside the Ark of the Covenant; and he placed the ark in the Most Holy Place.

God made it clear to Moses that Aaron and his sons, as the priests, would be the only ones who were to enter the Holy Place. Further, Aaron, as the high priest, would be the only one allowed to enter the Most Holy Place, and he could only enter it once a year on the Day of Atonement. The people could draw only so close to God. The priests would then cover the distance between the people and God, acting as the intermediary representing the people before God.

Since the Israelites were on a journey, the tabernacle needed to be able to move with them. Therefore, God gave Moses explicit instructions as to how to break down the tabernacle, pack all of its contents and move it. The tabernacle traveled with the Israelites throughout all the years they wandered in the wilderness. When the Israelites crossed the Jordan River into the promised land, they took the tabernacle with them. While the Israelite army was taking possession of each of the enemy cities, their main camp was at Gilgal. The tabernacle most likely remained at Gilgal until all the cities were conquered. It was then moved to Shiloh, where it remained throughout the three hundred or so years the Israelites went through their cyclical pattern of moving away from and returning to God.

One of the enemy nations that conquered and enslaved the Israelites during this time, the Philistines, captured the Ark of the Covenant during a battle. When this happened, King Saul moved the tabernacle to Nob, near his hometown. It was later moved to Gibeon. The Philistine leaders eventually returned the Ark of the Covenant to the Israelites. The ark was then kept in the town of Kiriath-jearim. The tabernacle, however, remained at Gibeon. When David became king he retrieved the ark and brought it to Jerusalem, where it was kept in a tent. The tabernacle, though, stayed in Gibeon.

> When David was settled in his palace, he summoned Nathan the prophet. "Look," David said, "I am living in a beautiful cedar palace, but the Ark of the LORD's Covenant is out there under a tent!"
>
> Nathan replied to David, "Do whatever you have in mind, for God is with you."
>
> But that same night God said to Nathan,
>
> "Go and tell my servant David, 'This is what the LORD has declared: You are not the one to build a house for me to live in. I have never lived in a house, from the day I brought the Israelites out of Egypt until this very day. My home has always been a tent, moving from one place to another in a Tabernacle.'" (1 Chronicles 17:1–5)

Upon learning of God's directive,
David said to Solomon:

"The LORD has chosen you to build a Temple as his sanctuary. Be strong, and do the work." Then David gave Solomon the plans for the Temple and its surroundings . . .

"Every part of this plan," David told Solomon, "was given to me in writing from the hand of the LORD." (1 Chronicles 28:10–11, 19)

It was in midspring, in the month of Ziv, during the fourth year of Solomon's reign, that he began to construct the Temple of the LORD. This was 480 years after the people of Israel were rescued from their slavery in the land of Egypt. (1 Kings 6:1)

And he made the Most Holy Place. It's length was according to the width of the house, twenty cubits, and its width twenty cubits. He overlaid it with six hundred talents of fine gold. The weight of the nails was fifty shekels of gold; and he overlaid the upper area with gold. In the Most Holy Place he made two cherubim, fashioned by carving, and overlaid them with gold. . . . The wings of these cherubim spanned twenty cubits overall. They stood on their feet, and they faced inward. And he made the veil of blue, purple, crimson, and fine linen and wove cherubim into it. (2 Chronicles 3:8–10, 13–14 NKJV)

The entire building was completed in every detail by midautumn, in the month of Bul, during the eleventh year of his reign. So it took seven years to build the Temple. (1 Kings 6:38)

Solomon then summoned to Jerusalem the elders of Israel and all the heads of the tribes—the leaders of the ancestral families of the Israelites. They were to bring the Ark of the LORD's covenant to the Temple . . .

When all the elders of Israel arrived, the priests picked up the Ark. The priests and Levites brought up the Ark of the LORD along with the special tent and all the sacred items that had been in it. There, before the Ark, King Solomon and the entire community of Israel sacrificed so many sheep, goats, and cattle that no one could keep count!

Then the priests carried the Ark of the LORD's covenant into the inner sanctuary of the Temple—the Most Holy Place—and placed it beneath the wings of the cherubim. . . . Nothing was in the Ark except the two stone tablets that Moses had placed in it at Mount Sinai, where the LORD made a covenant with the people of Israel when they left the Land of Egypt. (1 Kings 8:1, 3–6, 9)

As stated in chapter five, the temple was destroyed when God exiled the southern kingdom (Judah) to Babylon. When King Cyrus of Persia conquered the Babylonian empire, he permitted the people of Judah to return to Jerusalem and rebuild the temple.

"The construction of the Temple of God began in midspring, during the second year after they arrived in Jerusalem" (Ezra 3:8). Once the foundation was laid, "local residents tried to discourage and frighten the people of Judah to keep them from their work. They bribed agents to work against them and to frustrate their plans. This went on during the entire reign of King Cyrus of Persia and lasted until King Darius of Persia took the throne" (Ezra 4:4–5).

Work in the temple began again during the second year of King Darius's reign. King Darius supported the rebuilding of the temple by sending the following message to those who were trying to sabotage the building project:

> "Do not disturb the construction of the Temple of God. Let it be rebuilt on its original site, and do not hinder the governor of Judah and the elders of the Jews in their work. . . . Those who violate this decree in any way will have a beam pulled from their house. Then they will be lifted up and impaled on it, and their house will be reduced to a pile of rubble." (Ezra 6:7, 11)

The temple was completed during the sixth year of King Darius's reign. "The Temple of God was then dedicated with great joy by the people of Israel, the priests, the Levites, and the rest of the people who had returned from exile" (Ezra 6:16).

This is the temple that was standing in Jerusalem at the time of Jesus' death. When the veil in the temple ripped in half, it signified that the relationship between God and humanity was restored. The transition from the old covenant to the new covenant was complete. When God tore the veil in the temple he was, in essence, inviting people to come to him directly and enter into relationship with him. They no longer needed priests to act as intermediaries. Each individual now had direct access to God, if he or she wanted that.

God's invitation to enter into relationship with him still stands. Though God deeply desires a relationship with every human being he creates, he is respectful. He does not force himself on us. He doesn't demand or coerce. He invites.

It is important to remember that every one of us needs to make a decision whether to accept or reject God's invitation. It is also important to remember that not making a decision is, in essence, rejecting God's invitation for a relationship.

How to accept God's invitation

Accepting God's invitation for a relationship involves apologizing to God for behaviors and attitudes you engage in that are not in line with his values, stopping those behaviors and attitudes and turning toward God—aka, repenting. Turning toward God means beginning to live your life his way, aligning your behaviors and attitudes with his values.

For many of us, this is a process. Though giving your life to God, entering into relationship with him, accepting his free gift of forgiveness and salvation, deciding to live your life his way and turning toward him is a once in a lifetime decision, actually *living* your life his way is a lifetime process. Old habits die hard and usually don't give up without a fight. The more ingrained these attitudes and behaviors are, the longer it takes to change them and the more work and effort it will require. Once we are in relationship with God, however, the wonderful news is that we don't have to do it alone. He will be right there next to us, encouraging us, supporting us and helping us.

John the Baptist told us how to accept God's invitation: "Repent of your sins and turn to God" (Matthew 3:2). When Jesus began his earthly ministry, he echoed John the Baptist's words, instructing us how to accept God's invitation: "From then on Jesus began to preach, 'Repent of your sins and turn to God, for the Kingdom of Heaven is near'" (Matthew 4:17).

In his letter to the church in Rome, the apostle Paul urged the people of that church to accept God's invitation by committing their lives to Christ: "And so, dear brothers, I plead with you to give your bodies to God. Let them be a living sacrifice, holy—the kind he can accept. When you think of what he has done for you, is this too much to ask?" (Romans 12:1 TLB).

Paul is telling them, and us, what it means to commit our lives to Christ and how to do this. When he says "give your bodies to God," he is saying that God wants all of each one of us. Paul is telling us, as he was them, that God doesn't want only what we choose to give him; he wants his creation back in its entirety. God created each one of us for a specific purpose, and he equipped us to fulfill that purpose. What he wants in return is for each of us to surrender ourselves to him and allow him to use us as he chooses.

When Paul said "Let them be a living and holy sacrifice," he was explaining to the Christians in Rome that what is required under the new covenant is markedly different from what had been required under the old covenant. Paul was telling them that God no longer wants a dead sacrifice— i.e., animals burned on the altar of the tabernacle. God now wants a living sacrifice. He wants us to give *ourselves* to him so he can use us to further his work in the world.

Paul reminds us of the sacrifice God made for all (Christ's death on the cross) when he says, "When you think of what he has done for you, . . . " Paul is reminding his audience that God gave his only Son to experience a death marked by a degree of agony that few, if any, of us could even come close to imagining. Paul goes on to challenge both them and us with "Is this too much to ask?"

Personal sidebar: When you really think about the sacrifice Jesus made for us (he left the glory of heaven to enter the world in a human body and then allowed himself to be beaten beyond recognition, mocked, abused and then to die a slow, tortuous death on a wooden cross), is our full surrender indeed too much to ask?

When I accepted God's invitation

As described in chapter four, accepting God's invitation for a personal relationship with him through his Son, Jesus Christ, was, for me, not quick or easy. It was a rather long process during which I had to come to terms with the reality that many of the things I had been taught about God as I was growing up were simply not true. I wrestled with beliefs that I had embraced unquestioningly as a child and made decisions about whether to hold on to those beliefs or let go of them and embrace realities I was hearing about as an adult. As I stated, I decided in favor of new beliefs and began my walk with Jesus.

This process took place in the mid- to late 1990s. Though I had made the decision to give my life to God and live my life his way, and I knew that Jesus had died for me and that my sins were forgiven and I would go to heaven when I died, I didn't feel any different. I still struggled with ungodly behaviors and attitudes and felt directionless. I wanted to serve God and knew he had a particular plan as to how he wanted me to serve him; however, I didn't have the faintest idea what that plan was.

This all changed in the fall of 2002 following a worship service in which the preacher spoke about being ashamed of our relationship with Jesus. He looked at the congregation and emphatically stated, "Never be ashamed of your relationship with Jesus Christ!" I felt as though he was speaking right to me. I knew I had been a closet Christian. I went right home and got down on my knees and apologized to God for being ashamed of my relationship with his Son. I immediately felt adrenaline surge throughout my whole body, and God, right then and there, gave me a directive regarding something he wanted me to do for him. I did it, and he has been guiding and directing my steps ever since. He has also been taking care of me and healing me.

CHAPTER EIGHT

THE HEALING PLACE

Due to the dysfunction in the family I grew up in, I entered adulthood with many emotional and spiritual wounds, destructive habits and crippling hang-ups, most of which were outside my awareness. I began a healing process in my early adulthood even though I did not have a clear idea of what needed to be healed.

As stated in chapter three, the first step in my healing process was engaging in psychotherapy. Though I experienced healing while in therapy (also described in chapter three), psychotherapy did not fill my internal emptiness or give me a sense of being valuable and worthwhile. Psychotherapy helped me to change on the outside; my inside, however, remained untouched for a very long time. Without consciously realizing it, I accepted this as normal, assuming I had reached the end of the healing process.

While still in therapy I added secular recovery (ACOA ALANON) to my healing process. Secular recovery taught me that I was not alone. I learned firsthand that other people had life experiences similar to mine and had similar feelings to mine. This was immensely comforting to me and helped to heal the aloneness. It didn't take me the distance, though; I was still left with a sense of emptiness and did not feel valuable or worthwhile.

In 2003 I stumbled upon Celebrate Recovery, a Christ-centered 12-Step recovery program, and that has made all the difference for me. Through working a program that continually pointed me toward Jesus, I learned how to access his healing power. My childhood wounds were finally healed—not coped with but *healed*. My habits are being broken one by one, and my crippling hang-ups have evaporated. They have been replaced with faith and trust in my Higher Power, Jesus Christ.

My spiritual wounds began to be healed during my time of spiritual re-education described in chapter four. Working the Celebrate Recovery program completed the healing process. It took me the distance. Through working the Christ-centered 12 Steps in Celebrate Recovery I learned that my worth and value come solely from being a child of God. It taught me that the healing place is my relationship with God, as personified in Jesus Christ. I belong to him and know that he will never abandon me or forsake me. I don't have to please others or gain others' approval in order for God to love me. He loves me no matter what, and he knew me and loved me before he placed me in my mother's womb. There is nothing I can do to make him love me, and there is nothing I can do to make him not love me. His love for me is not based on what I do or who I am. It is based on who *he is*. Feeling secure in his love, I now gratefully live my life for him. I am no longer bound by a sick need to please human beings and obtain their approval. I am living my life for an audience of One.

Paths to healing

There are a variety of paths one can take to heal emotional and/or spiritual wounds. Since therapy and recovery were the paths that I chose, and that worked for me, I would like to discuss each in depth.

Before doing so, however, I would like to make sure that the terms being used are clearly understood. When I speak about therapy, I am referring specifically to secular psychotherapy with a trained and licensed professional (psychologist, clinical social worker, professional counselor or psychiatrist). I am not referring to any particular school of thought regarding therapy or to any particular therapeutic approach, technique or method. Recovery refers specifically to Christ-centered recovery. Though it is beyond question that countless numbers of people have been helped through secular 12-Step groups, the focus here is Christ-centered recovery.

Important note: This book is not about the power of a group or the effectiveness of a program. It is about the inner transformations that occur when one is in relationship with Jesus Christ. Celebrate Recovery, or any other Christ-centered recovery program, is not the answer. Jesus is the answer. Celebrate Recovery is merely one of the channels through which Jesus works. It is one avenue through which people are led into relationship with Jesus and can experience his healing power.

Therapy and recovery exist for similar reasons and have similar goals—i.e., growth, change, improved functioning, healthier relationships and so forth. The ways in which they accomplish these goals, however, are quite different, as are the underlying beliefs regarding how change happens.

It is my belief that most, if not all, of the problems for which people seek therapy and/or enter recovery have their roots in toxic shame. In order for true and lasting change to take place, therefore, that toxic shame must be healed.

As discussed at length in chapter two, toxic shame grows out of the lack of health of our families and primary caretaker(s) and develops in a child when he or she does not experience unconditional love. It would seem to make sense, then, that in order for the toxic shame to be healed the critical ingredient that must be present is unconditional love.

Due to this premise, the central question that will be addressed as the differences between therapy and recovery are explored and discussed is: Which is more effective at imparting unconditional love and thereby healing toxic shame—therapy or recovery?

Before we begin looking at the differences between therapy and recovery, though, we will look at one similarity. That similarity is that both occur within the context of relationship. Therapy obviously takes place within the context of a relationship, and the quality of the therapist-client relationship is a critical determining factor in the success or failure of the therapy. Recovery also takes place within the context of relationship. The human relationships in recovery are extremely valuable and contribute immensely to the healing. Everyone is struggling and walking the road to recovery. Though individuals may have different recovery issues, no one is any better than anyone else. In addition, as one establishes his or her relationship with Jesus Christ and grows in that relationship, one is in the place where true healing happens.

Looking at effectiveness

Though therapy takes place within the context of relationship, the therapist-client relationship is characterized by some inherent factors that impact therapy's effectiveness at healing toxic shame.

First, the therapist-client relationship is, by its very nature, unequal. The therapist is seen as "an expert," and the client pays the therapist for that expertise. The therapist also tends to be seen as emotionally and mentally healthy. Whether or not this perception is accurate is irrelevant. What is relevant is that this is the perception the client operates from. The client, on the other hand, is seen by the therapist, as well as by himself or herself, as sick, troubled and dysfunctional. This automatically puts the client in a one-down position vis-à-vis the therapist. This one-down position is maintained by such therapeutic tools as diagnoses and treatment plans. Diagnoses reinforce the concept that the client is sick, and treatment plans maintain the client's one-down position vis-à-vis the therapist; i.e., the "healthy" therapist is "treating" the "unhealthy" client. George Weinberg, in his book *The Heart of Psychotherapy*, puts it this way: "The very nature of the relationship is that of a success talking to a failure."[26]

Point to ponder: When one recalls that a person's toxic shame develops in childhood within the context of the child's dependent relationship with his or her parent(s) or caretaker(s), one would wonder if that toxic shame could be healed within the context of such an unequal relationship.

Second, human beings, due to an imperfect human nature, are unable to love one another with perfect, unconditional love. Psychotherapists, in spite of degrees, training, experience and licenses, are still human beings with all the limits, flaws and imperfections inherent in being human. They are, then, unable to love another with perfect, unconditional love. They also, for the most part, do not see their job as loving their clients. They see their job as fixing their damaged, sick, dysfunctional clients.

Another point to ponder: Since the essence of toxic shame is a belief that one is inadequate and insufficient in an unfixable way, the question naturally arises as to how one's toxic shame can be healed within the context of a relationship in which one is seen as sick, dysfunctional, etc.

The relationships among individuals in recovery, on the other hand, are equal relationships. All are struggling and walking the road to recovery, and all are sharing their struggles openly. Therapist self-disclosure is used as a therapeutic tool to help the sick, dysfunctional client and is meant to be occasional. Individuals in recovery share as a necessary part of their recovery, not to help anyone else, thus underscoring the equality of the relationships.

Another factor that underscores the equality of the relationships in recovery and the inequality of the therapist-client relationship is that recovery leaders are expected to be continually working on their own recoveries. The same expectation is not present for therapists. In all my years working as a mental health professional, I never once encountered an expectation by employers, supervisors or licensing boards that I work on my own mental health, thus giving rise to the assumption, accurate or not, that the therapist is emotionally and mentally healthy.

To summarize this section, it is my belief that the inherent imbalance in power and the perceived imbalance in health of the therapist-client relationship tends to increase toxic shame rather than decrease it. The equality evident in the relationships between recovery participants and recovery leaders contributes to the healing of the toxic shame. Sharing who one is and what one struggles with in a group of people who share similar struggles counteracts the feeling of isolation and the belief that one is different. When one experiences that he or she is not the only one who feels like this, has done these things or has experienced these struggles, the reality of knowing that you are not alone sinks in and goes a long way toward healing toxic shame. When this is coupled with feeling loved and accepted for who you are by the One who loves with perfect love, toxic shame doesn't have a chance.

The apostle Paul tried to convey the immense scope of God's love in his letters. To the church in Ephesus, he wrote:

> And may you have the power to understand, as all God's people should, how wide, how long, how high, and how deep his love is. May you experience the love of Christ, though it is too

great to understand fully. Then you will be made complete with all the fullness of life and power that comes from God. (Ephesians 3:18–19)

To the church in Rome, he wrote:

And I am convinced that nothing can ever separate us from God's love. Neither death nor life, neither angels nor demons, neither our fears for today nor our worries about tomorrow–not even the powers of hell can separate us from God's love. No power in the sky above or in the earth below–indeed, nothing in all creation will ever be able to separate us from the love of God that is revealed in Christ Jesus our Lord. (Romans 8:38–39)

How does healing happen?

The question "How does healing happen?" leads to an exploration of a critical difference in belief systems between therapy and recovery.

One of the underlying beliefs in therapy is that the patient or the client has the power within to heal the self. The role of the therapist is to facilitate this healing process. The belief in recovery, on the other hand, is that the individual is powerless to heal himself. This admission of powerlessness is believed to be critical and foundational. It is believed that until one takes the first step of admitting one's powerlessness, recovery cannot begin and change will not happen. In recovery, the healer is believed to be our Higher Power, Jesus Christ. It is this admission of powerlessness that opens oneself up to Christ's healing touch.

Therapy is about empowering the client to meet her own needs and to make necessary changes. Recovery is about maintaining an attitude of powerlessness and learning to turn to God for the strength and power to change. A turning point in my own recovery was when I truly understood and embraced the recovery saying, "It's not willpower—it's God power."

If one accepts the premise that most, if not all, of the problems for which people seek therapy and/or enter recovery have their roots in toxic shame, then one would logically and automatically believe that people in therapy and/or recovery did not have their needs met in childhood, particularly their need to be loved unconditionally. Therapy's response to this (due to the underlying belief that the client has the power within to heal herself) is to teach the client to parent the self. Recovery's response (due to the underlying belief that the individual is powerless to heal himself) is to encourage the individual to turn to God, our heavenly Parent, for parenting.

This difference between the two belief systems became blatantly clear to me during a meeting I attended while still working as a mental health professional. Present at the meeting were seven therapists, including myself. We were talking about working with clients who were abused or neglected as children. The focus of the discussion was how to teach the clients to parent themselves. As I sat at the table listening to the discussion taking place around me, I felt depressed and frustrated in reaction to my colleagues' lack of awareness of their heavenly Father and their failure to teach clients to turn to him for parenting rather than turning to self. A very deep sorrow welled up inside me as I continued to listen to my colleagues describe how they were teaching their clients to lean on "themselves" and "parent themselves" rather than to run into the arms of their heavenly Father. My sorrow grew out of my memory of how isolated and alone I had felt when I trusted in myself and my abilities, when I was self-reliant rather than God-reliant.

In my opinion, when therapists teach clients to parent themselves, they inadvertently foster feelings of emptiness, aloneness and disconnection and, without meaning to, feed toxic shame rather than help to eliminate it. It has been my experience that those of us who were deeply hurt in childhood are unable to heal our own hurts. The hurts are too massive, too pervasive. When I turned to myself to try to parent myself, I was unsuccessful in doing that. I had an intellectual understanding of what had happened in my family and the wounds I had incurred because of that. I was not able to heal those wounds, however, because I simply did not have what it took inside me to heal them. I was not able to love myself unconditionally because I had no experience of being loved unconditionally. What was inside me was toxic shame. How can toxic shame heal toxic shame?

An important difference

Another important difference between therapy and recovery involves the concept of forgiveness. In therapy, one is encouraged to resolve issues related to people who have hurt us and to change behaviors that hurt self and others. In recovery, one is encouraged to forgive people who have hurt us and to ask for forgiveness from people we have hurt.

During my time of working as a psychotherapist, forgiveness was not in my repertoire of therapeutic strategies and techniques. I have no memory of ever hearing forgiveness mentioned when I was in graduate school learning how to be a therapist. I also have no memory of ever hearing about forgiveness during my years as a client in therapy. As far as I can recollect, the need for me to forgive those who had hurt me, the need to ask forgiveness from the people I had hurt, and the need to forgive myself were never mentioned. Therefore, it was no wonder that in my work as a psychotherapist forgiveness was not on my radar screen.

Though the world of mental health and behavioral sciences has not historically considered forgiveness to be important, other segments of the population consider it to be very important. In October 2006 the world witnessed one of the clearest and most moving examples of forgiveness in recent history. This example was provided by the Amish people of Lancaster County, Pennsylvania, as they responded to the shooting of ten Amish schoolgirls.

On October 2, 2006, thirty-two-year-old Charles Carl Roberts IV entered a one-room Amish schoolhouse in rural southern Lancaster County armed with a semi-automatic pistol. Inside the schoolhouse were twenty-six children, aged six to thirteen, their twenty-year-old female teacher, and four guests—the teacher's mother, sister, and two sisters-in-law. One of the young women had two small children with her. As Roberts was entering the schoolhouse, the teacher, her mother, and a nine-year-old girl slipped out a side door. The teacher ran a quarter of a mile to a farmhouse, from which she phoned 911. Roberts told the other adults and the boys to leave the building. He was then alone with ten girls. State troopers arrived shortly thereafter and surrounded the locked schoolhouse. When the police heard gunshots inside the schoolhouse, they forced their way into the building. Roberts had shot all ten girls and then killed himself. Five of the girls died. The others were critically injured.

Forgiveness at work

The response of the Amish people to this horrific tragedy, particularly the response of the parents whose daughters had been killed or critically injured, baffled the world. They forgave Roberts for what he had done and manifested that forgiveness in actions as well as words. They visited Roberts's widow (Amy), his children, and his parents. During these visits they expressed much comfort, concern, condolences and forgiveness. They also attended Roberts's funeral.

To the Amish forgiveness is simply a way of life. That the outside world was surprised by Amish forgiveness in turn surprised the Amish. "Why is everybody all surprised?" asked one Amish man. "It's just standard Christian forgiveness; it's what everybody should be doing." An Amish woman was similarly taken aback by the national attention their forgiveness had generated. "Before the media made such a big deal of forgiveness, I never realized that it was so much a part of our life. I just never realized before how central it is to us."[27]

These statements were taken from the book *Amish Grace; How Forgiveness Transcended Tragedy* by Donald Kraybill, Steven Nolt and David Weaver-Zercher. They provide a window into a possible explanation as to why forgiveness has not until recently been incorporated into the study and practice of professional mental health services. Forgiveness is not a strategy or technique that one can pull out when needed. It is deeply rooted in one's values and lifestyle. In order to practice true forgiveness when needed, the importance of forgiveness and the willingness to forgive need to be intricately woven into one's belief system—hence the stumbling block to incorporating forgiveness into therapy; i.e., therapy solves problems where recovery teaches a lifestyle.

Another factor that may have contributed to why forgiveness has historically not been incorporated into therapy practices is that it flies in the face of cultural or worldly values and norms that are embedded in us as individuals and as a society. A relative of the deceased killer in Lancaster County summed up this point succinctly when he remarked, "If this had happened to some of our own [non-Amish] people, there would have been one lawsuit after another."[28]

In summary, when one is struggling with emotional and/or spiritual wounds, destructive habits and/or crippling hang-ups that are impeding one's life and are most probably rooted in toxic shame, three available avenues for healing are psychotherapy, secular recovery and Christ-centered recovery. Though therapy and secular recovery undeniably help people to change for the better, it has been my experience that neither one can take you the distance. Only God, personified in Jesus Christ, can love with perfect, unconditional love, and because of this he is the only one who can heal toxic shame. Therefore, a program such as Celebrate Recovery that acknowledges God as the healer and is continually pointing people toward God for their healing is the most effective at healing toxic shame.

John Bradshaw, in his book *Healing the Shame that Binds You*, states:

> Twelve-step groups literally were born out of the courage of two people risking coming out of hiding. One alcoholic person (Bill W.) turned to another alcoholic person (Dr. Bob) and they told each other how bad they really felt about themselves. I join with Scott Peck in seeing this dialogue coming out of hiding as one of the most important events of this century.[29]

I join with John Bradshaw and Scott Peck in seeing the dialogue between Bill W. and Dr. Bob, in which they each came out of hiding and gave birth to 12-Step groups, as one of the most important events of the 20th century. I believe that another important event of the 20th century, a building block on what Bill W. and Dr. Bob did, is what John Baker and Rick Warren did. John Baker understood the vision God gave him for a Christ-centered recovery program and acted on it, giving birth to Celebrate Recovery. Rick Warren gave John Baker the needed permission and support to establish and build Celebrate Recovery at Saddleback Church in Southern California and then take it to the world.

More on healing

When God designed our bodies, he instilled in us a natural healing process for when we get injured or sick. Just watch the way a cut heals for an example of this.

The healing process doesn't always happen in the way or the timing that we want, though. This is because we are not in charge of our own healing—God is. The healing is God's choice, it's always God's choice. For example, God may choose not to heal the physical or mental illness. He may choose, instead, to give us the inner strength, peace and resources to cope with the illness.

When it comes to emotional and spiritual wounds, however, I believe that God wants to heal us. I believe he wants to heal us so we can be effective instruments in furthering his work in the world in the specific way he has chosen for us to do that. In his book *The Purpose Driven Life* Rick Warren states, "Before God created you, he decided what role he wanted you to play on earth. He planned exactly how he wanted you to serve him, and then he shaped you for those tasks. You are the way you are because you were made for a specific ministry."[30]

God wants us to fulfill the purpose he chose for us, and he wants us to fulfill it effectively. Therefore, he gave us the skills, abilities, talents and gifts we would need to fulfill that purpose. In addition, he gave us a passion to do it. By giving us everything we need to fulfill his purpose for our life, he wired us to succeed. We will not succeed, however, if we are unhealthy emotionally and/or spiritually. Therefore, if we want to successfully walk in God's specific will for our lives, it is imperative that we allow God to heal our emotional and spiritual wounds.

Remember, though, as stated in chapter seven, that God is respectful. Just as he doesn't force his invitations for relationship on us, he doesn't force his healing on us. He gave us free will. This means that we have the power to make choices, and the choices that we make can either allow God to heal us or hinder him from healing us. Our choices can either facilitate the natural healing process or block it.

The first choice we have to make, believe it or not, is deciding whether we want to get well. As hard as this is for some people to believe, not everyone wants to get well. We can become so comfortable with our wounds, destructive habits and crippling hang-ups that we don't want to live without them. They become part of our identity. Though they may get in the way in some area or areas of life, they may be our best friends or protectors in other areas.

> Afterward Jesus returned to Jerusalem for one of the Jewish holy days. Inside the city, near the Sheep Gate, was the pool of Bethesda, with five covered porches. Crowds of sick people—blind, lame, or paralyzed—lay on the porches. One of the men lying there had been sick for thirty-eight years. When Jesus saw him and knew he had been ill for a long time, he asked him, "Would you like to get well?" (John 5:1–6).

The next choice we have to make is this: Are we willing to do whatever it takes to get well? Sometimes there are things we need to do, doctors we need to see, medicines we need to take, procedures we need to undergo, therapy sessions we need to go to, recovery meetings we need to attend, etc., in order to get well. The question then becomes whether we are willing to do whatever is needed.

Broken, hurting, struggling people sought out Jesus. The Bible is full of stories of people who flocked to him, followed him, chased him down and conquered obstacles to get to him.

> Soon the house where he was staying was so packed with visitors that there was no more room, even outside the door. While he was preaching God's word to them, four men arrived carrying a paralyzed man on a mat.
>
> They couldn't bring him to Jesus because of the crowd, so they dug a hole through the roof above his head. Then they lowered the man on his mat, right down in front of Jesus (Mark 2:2–4).

Why did they go to such lengths? They knew he loved them, they knew he could heal them, and they felt safe enough to go to him. The same is true today. Emotional and spiritual wounds can be healed in a personal relationship with God through Jesus Christ.

Final note on the 12 Steps

The 12 Steps were developed by Bill W. and Dr. Bob as a path to recovery when they founded Alcoholics Anonymous in the 1930s. Many people believe that the 12 Steps were divinely inspired and, indeed, Bill W. developed them following a spiritual experience he had in which his desire to drink alcohol was removed. When you read the 12 Steps and *really* think about them, they are a roadmap to God and guidelines for living a Christian life.

If you are not familiar with the 12 Steps and/or do not understand how they could be a roadmap for living a Christian life, go to Appendix Five.

CHAPTER NINE

NURTURING THE RELATIONSHIP

Any relationship, if it is to be healthy and vibrant, needs to be nurtured. This is true not only of our human relationships but also holds true for our relationship with God. Just as plants need to be nurtured with sun and water in order to stay alive and to grow, our relationship with God needs to be nurtured in order to live and grow. The sun and water of our relationship with God are prayer and worship.

Prayer is the sun

"As often as possible Jesus withdrew to out-of-the-way places for prayer" (Luke 5:16 MSG).

Jesus is our primary model for developing and maintaining a healthy prayer life. Throughout his earthly ministry Jesus frequently spent time with his Father in prayer. It is what kept him going. It gave him the fuel he needed to carry out his mission on earth.

When Jesus prayed he talked to his Father the way any one of us would talk to someone we trusted, respected and cared deeply about. He did not recite memorized words and phrases. He told his Father how he felt and what he needed. For example, when Jesus arrived at the tomb of his friend Lazarus he told those who were present to roll the stone aside from the entrance to the tomb.

> So they rolled the stone aside. Then Jesus looked up to heaven and said, "Father, thank you for hearing me. You always hear me, but I said it out loud for the sake of all these people standing here, so that they will believe you sent me." Then Jesus shouted, "Lazarus, come out!" And the dead man came out, his hands and feet bound in graveclothes, his face wrapped in a headcloth. Jesus told them, "Unwrap him and let him go!" (John 11:41–44)

Another example of Jesus engaging in authentic dialogue with his Father was when he prayed in the Garden of Gethsemane immediately prior to his arrest:

> "Father, if you are willing, please take this cup of suffering away from me. Yet I want your will to be done, not mine." Then an angel from heaven appeared and strengthened him. He prayed more fervently, and he was in such agony of spirit that his sweat fell to the ground like great drops of blood. (Luke 22:42–44)

Jesus was real with his Father. He did not pretend to feel something he did not feel, nor did he minimize how he was feeling. This is an example to us. God wants us to be as real with him as Jesus was.

A different experience

Growing up, my experience of prayer was very different from what Jesus modeled. I was taught to memorize prayers someone else had written and then to recite those prayers at specified times during liturgies. As these prayers were never explained to me, I had no understanding of what the words and phrases I was reciting meant. I was not connected to these prayers in any way. The entire experience of praying was empty and meaningless to me.

As my personal relationship with God grew and developed, I began to see prayer in a new and very different light. I began to experience prayer as a relational dialogue. I could talk to the God of the universe, and he talked to me! What an awesome privilege! He actually cared enough about me and my life to listen and respond.

Note: God's communications to me did not come in the form of audible words. They came in a multitude of other forms. Sometimes they would come as internal promptings and feelings that I knew were from the Holy Spirit. Other times they would come in the form of words practically jumping off a page at me as I read the Bible, or words of a worship song I was listening to touching me in a deep and powerful way. Still other times God chose to speak to me through people. Regardless of the form God's communications came in, each one was accompanied by a sensing or a knowing in the very fiber of my being that God was telling me something.

Learning to pray

As I worked at my prayer life I encountered several difficulties and obstacles. First of all, due to my childhood experience of prayer I was resistant to formulas for prayer. Because of this I did not avail myself of help that was offered to me to develop a prayer life. I was afraid that I would be put into a religious straitjacket. I did not want my prayer life to be another empty exercise. I wanted it to be real and vibrant. Though I wanted this and indeed yearned for it, I was also afraid of it. I had not experienced this kind of dialogue growing up in my family and, therefore, as I moved into adulthood engaging in a dialogue in which I could be totally honest and vulnerable was not familiar to me or comfortable for me. I struggled with this in both my human relationships and in my relationship with God.

As I got to know God and understand his character, I was able to see the differences between my heavenly Parent and my earthly parents. I came to realize and believe that though my earthly parents had not engaged in this kind of authentic dialogue with me, my heavenly Parent was different. He wanted authentic dialogue, not superficial chatter.

Another obstacle I encountered as I was learning to pray was truly believing that prayer moves the hand of God. Though I wanted to believe this, down deep inside me I really did not believe that my prayers made a difference to God at all, that they would have any impact on what he chose to do or not do. Not only did I have difficulty believing that my prayers could move the hand of God, I felt guilty for having difficulty believing this. My guilt decreased somewhat when I read the following Scripture passage from Acts 12:3–16:

Herod . . . arrested Peter. . . . Then he imprisoned him, placing him under the guard of four squads of four soldiers each. Herod intended to bring Peter out for public trial after the Passover. But while Peter was in prison, the church prayed very earnestly for him.

The night before Peter was to be placed on trial, he was asleep, fastened with two chains between two soldiers. Others stood guard at the prison gate. Suddenly, there was a bright light in the cell, and an angel of the Lord stood before Peter. The angel struck him on the side to awaken him and said, "Quick! Get up!" And the chains fell off his wrists. Then the angel told him, "Get dressed and put on your sandals." And he did. "Now put on your coat and follow me," the angel ordered.

So Peter left the cell, following the angel. But all the time he thought it was a vision. He didn't realize it was actually happening. They passed the first and second guard posts and came to the iron gate leading to the city, and this opened for them all by itself. So they passed through and started walking down the street, and then the angel suddenly left him.

Peter finally came to his senses. "It's really true!" he said. "The Lord has sent his angel and saved me from Herod and from what the Jewish leaders had planned to do to me!"

When he realized this, he went to the home of Mary, the mother of John Mark, where many were gathered for prayer. He knocked at the door in the gate, and a servant girl named Rhoda came to open it. When she recognized Peter's voice, she was so overjoyed that, instead of opening the door she ran back inside and told everyone, "Peter is standing at the door!"

"You're out of your mind!" they said. When she insisted, they decided, "It must be his angel."

Meanwhile, Peter continued knocking. When they finally opened the door and saw him, they were amazed.

Why didn't they believe Rhoda? Why were they amazed when they saw Peter standing at the door? Scripture tells us that they had been praying for him. I imagine many, if not all, of the prayers were for his release. When Rhoda told them that Peter was standing at the door, why didn't they reply "Of course he is. We've been praying for this." Could it be that they also did not fully believe in the power of prayer?

I don't know who all was gathered at the home of Mary, the mother of John Mark; however, I have to believe that at least some of those who were gathered there knew Jesus in the flesh. Some may very well have even traveled with him. So when I think of my difficulty believing in the power of prayer I am comforted by the knowledge that even people who knew Jesus in the flesh and probably watched him praying and probably listened to his teachings on prayer also had trouble believing in the power of prayer.

Any of you reading this who have had or are still having difficulty believing that prayer moves the hand of God, I hope that you can take some comfort in knowing that you are in good company.

More encouragement

I was further encouraged and emboldened when I read the following words of Jesus to his disciples as he was teaching them about prayer:

> "And so I tell you, keep on asking, and you will receive what you ask for. Keep on seeking, and you will find. Keep on knocking, and the door will be opened to you. For everyone who asks, receives. Everyone who seeks, finds. And to everyone who knocks, the door will be opened.
>
> "You fathers—if your children ask for a fish, do you give them a snake instead? Or if they ask for an egg, do you give them a scorpion? Of course not! So if you sinful people know how to give good gifts to your children, how much more will your heavenly Father give the Holy Spirit to those who ask him." (Luke 11:9–13)

I decided to take Jesus at his word and do what he was telling us to do. I began to ask God for the desires of my heart and to tell him anything and everything that was on my mind. Though I have not received everything I have asked for, I trust that God hears me and, as a good Parent, considers everything that I ask for and answers my prayers in the way that he deems is best for me.

Bill Hybels's words in *Too Busy Not to Pray* further bolstered my efforts to learn to pray: "The important thing is not to follow a particular method but to find a way that works for you. Custom-design an approach that will still your racing mind and body, soften your heart and enable you to hear God's still, small voice. Then, when you are centered and focused on God, invite him to speak to you."[31]

I decided to heed Bill Hybels's advice as well and began to experiment with various ways to pray. I let go of my belief that there is a "right" way to pray—i.e., a "right" posture (kneeling), "right" words (a pre-written prayer), a "right" time" (first thing in the morning), and so forth. I embraced the belief that God doesn't care how I talk to him or when I talk to him. What he cares about is *that* I talk to him. I tried praying at different times during the day and in different places. I eventually found that though I had quiet times with God when I would sit quietly in his presence, what worked the best for me was to have an ongoing dialogue with him throughout each day as I lived my life. I began to talk to God while I was driving, walking, working, doing chores around the house, sitting on a bench in the mall waiting for one of my children and so forth. The possibilities were endless. I was reminded of Paul's words to the church in Thessalonica: "Pray without ceasing" (1 Thessalonians 5:17 NKJV).

I also found an additional role model for prayer. I began to look to Hannah in the Old Testament as another model for how to pray.

Once after a sacrificial meal at Shiloh, Hannah got up and went to pray. Eli the priest was sitting at his customary place beside the entrance of the Tabernacle. . . .

As she was praying to the LORD, Eli watched her. Seeing her lips moving but hearing no sound, he thought she had been drinking. "Must you come here drunk?" he demanded. "Throw away your wine!"

"Oh no, sir!" she replied. "I haven't been drinking wine or anything stronger. But I am very discouraged, and I was pouring out my heart to the LORD." (1 Samuel 1:9–10, 12–15)

The more I poured out my heart to God as Hannah did, the more he responded to me. As this exchange repeated itself over and over again, my relationship with God became more vibrant, firmly rooting itself in the center of my life. I began to see prayer not as an activity but rather as a lifestyle. An ongoing dialogue with God wove itself into the very fabric of my daily life and became as automatic to me as breathing. My need to stay connected to God became as much of a basic need as eating, sleeping and breathing. Over the years I have come to depend on him to keep going as much as I depend on air and water to keep living. It is the time I spend with God in prayer that breathes life into my relationship with him, and because he has consistently sustained me and provided for me I can't help but worship him.

Bill Hybels puts it this way: "Prayer is the way to turn dry, theological descriptions into warm, living, personal realities. When we live in constant communion with God, our needs are met, our faith increases, our love expands. We begin to feel God's peace in our hearts, and we spontaneously worship him."[32]

Worship is the water

As stated in chapter seven, King David retrieved the Ark of the Covenant from Kiriath-jearim and brought it to Jerusalem. When the ark entered the city of Jerusalem, "David danced before the LORD with all his might, wearing a priestly garment" (2 Samuel 6:14).

Though David was far from perfect, he loved God with all his heart, and that love spilled out when the ark entered Jerusalem. He was so full of joy to see the ark entering the Israelite capital city that his joy could not be contained and he danced (i.e., worshiped) *"with all his might."*

King David's worship was exuberant. It was fueled by his relationship with God and was a reflection of that relationship. It was also fueled by his understanding of the significance of the ark and his gratitude for what God had done for his people, the Israelites, through the ark.

Role of the ark

When the Israelites' time of wandering in the wilderness came to an end and they arrived at the land God had promised Abraham that he would give to his descendants, the ark played a significant role in the people's crossing of the Jordan River into the promised land.

"In the morning Joshua said to the priests, 'Lift up the Ark of the Covenant and lead the people across the river.' And so they started out and went ahead of the people" (Joshua 3:6). Joshua then said to the people:

"Look, the Ark of the Covenant, which belongs to the Lord of the whole earth, will lead you across the Jordan River! . . . The priests will carry the Ark of the Lord, the Lord of all the earth. As soon as their feet touch the water, the flow of the water will be cut off upstream, and the river will stand up like a wall."

So the people left their camp to cross the Jordan, and the priests who were carrying the Ark of the Covenant went ahead of them. It was the harvest season, and the Jordan was overflowing its banks. But as soon as the feet of the priests who were carrying the Ark touched the water at the river's edge, the water above that point began backing up a great distance away at a town called Adam, which is near Zarethan. And the water below that point flowed on to the Dead Sea until the riverbed was dry. Then all the people crossed over near the town of Jericho.

Meanwhile, the priests who were carrying the Ark of the Lord's Covenant stood on dry ground in the middle of the riverbed as the people passed by. They waited there until the whole nation of Israel had crossed the Jordan on dry ground (Joshua 3:11, 13–17).

And when everyone was safely on the other side, the priests crossed over with the Ark of the Lord as the people watched. . . .

As soon as the priests carrying the Ark of the Lord's Covenant came up out of the riverbed and their feet were on high ground, the water of the Jordan returned and overflowed its banks as before. (Joshua 4:11, 18)

After the Israelites entered the promised land they were faced with many walled cities full of enemies. The first was Jericho. Once again the ark played a significant role in the conquering of Jericho. The Lord gave the following instructions to Joshua as to how the army should proceed in order to capture Jericho:

> "You and your fighting men should march around the town once a day for six days. Seven priests will walk ahead of the Ark, each carrying a ram's horn. On the seventh day you are to march around the town seven times, with the priests blowing the horns. When you hear the priests give one long blast on the rams' horns, have all the people shout as loud as they can. Then the walls of the town will collapse, and the people can charge straight into the town." (Joshua 6:3–5)

Joshua did exactly as the Lord commanded him. Each day for six days the ark was carried around the walled city of Jericho, with seven priests walking in front of it, each carrying a ram's horn.

On the seventh day the Israelites got up at dawn and marched around the town as they had done before. But this time they went around the town seven times. The seventh time around, as the priests sounded the long blast on their horns,

Joshua commanded the people, "Shout! For the
LORD has given you the town!"...
    When the people heard the sound of the
rams' horns, they shouted as loud as they could.
Suddenly, the walls of Jericho collapsed, and the
Israelites charged straight into the town and
captured it. (Joshua 6:15–16, 20)

One by one the Israelites captured each of the enemy
cities. While the tabernacle most likely remained at Gilgal
during this process, the ark traveled with the Israelites,
playing a significant role in each victory. Eventually the
Israelites, led by Joshua, overcame their enemies and
possessed the land.

Other reactions

Not everyone worshipped and rejoiced as David did when
the ark entered Jerusalem. David's wife, Michal, did not
share in his joy. Rather than participating in the joyous
worship, Michal judged David's behavior and reacted with
loathing. "But as the Ark of the LORD entered the City of
David, Michal, the daughter of Saul, looked down from her
window. When she saw King David leaping and dancing
before the LORD, she was filled with contempt for him"
(2 Samuel 6:16).

    What fueled Michal's reaction is a matter of speculation
and is beyond the scope of this book. What is within the
bounds of this book, however, is the reality that though this
scenario occurred many centuries ago I have seen the same
dynamic at play in churches and at worship services today. I

have watched as some people worshiped God with joy and abandon while others looked at them with discomfort and/or disdain. Further, for a long time I allowed these looks of discomfort and disdain to stop me from freely worshipping God during a worship service.

In order to get past this and become free to worship during a church service, I had to come face-to-face with my codependent characteristic of caring about what people think of me and basing my opinion of myself on my perception of others' opinions about me. I not only had to come face-to-face with this character trait, I had to overcome it and not let it rule me. I overcame it by continually reminding myself that I am living my life for an audience of One and that his opinion of me is the only opinion that matters.

It is the time I spend worshipping God as the Spirit moves me that pumps blood into my relationship with him. I believe that God smiles when we allow ourselves to be who he created us to be. So when I worship him freely in a worship service, whether that be standing or sitting, or with hands raised or in my lap, and live the rest of my life with excellence, I know he is pleased.

Ingredients of Worship

Our worship of God, like David's, is grounded in our relationship with him and flows out of that relationship. It is also grounded in our understanding of what God has done for us. To truly worship God we must:

1. know God,
2. understand what he has done for us and
3. be grateful for what he has done for us.

Worship requires both our heart and our mind. It does not require musicians, a worship team, words on a screen or anything of the kind. In order for David to worship God with such exuberance as the ark was entering Jerusalem, David had to have a full understanding of what the ark meant in the history of his people (his mind), as well as deep appreciation and gratitude for the work God had done through the ark (his heart). In order for any one of us to truly worship God today, we must understand the significance of what Jesus did on the cross (mind) and have claimed Jesus' work on the cross as a personal gift, gratefully entering into a relationship with him (heart). It doesn't end there, though. One must also be an active participant in that relationship, relating to God day in and day out, understanding that God is alive and well and aware of how God is actively at work in each of our lives today.

Definitions of worship

Just as each person's relationship with God is individualized, each person's worship of God is also individualized and is not limited to how one behaves in a church service. Worship is far more than that. Worship is a lifestyle. "So whether you eat or drink, or whatever you do, do it all for the glory of God" (1 Corinthians 10:31).

In *The Purpose Driven Life* Rick Warren states, "Anything you do that brings pleasure to God is an act of worship."[33] He expands on this definition of worship in the foreword to *The Worship Answer Book* by Rick Muchow: "A simple definition of worship, based on the Great Commandment: Worship is any expression of our love to God —for who he is, what he has said, and what he's doing."[34] Joyce Meyer's definition of worship is as follows: "Worship is born in our hearts; it fills our thoughts and it is expressed through our mouths and through our bodies."[35] She goes on to say that

> When we read about worship in the Bible, we are reading about a personal relationship, about spiritual intimacy, and about passionate expressions of devotion from people who love and worship God with all of their hearts. This is true worship—the kind that bubbles up out of us when we have the fire of God in our lives, when our love for Him spills out all over everything, and when we are zealous and enthusiastic about our dynamic relationship with Him.[36]

When you think about worship this way it becomes obvious that our whole life, not just our behavior in a church service, can be lived as an act of worship.

CHAPTER TEN

THE BODY OF CHRIST

Up to this point I have focused exclusively on an individual's personal relationship with God. Though having a personal relationship with God is beyond important, it is also important to remember that God never meant for any of us to travel through life alone. He designed a system of interdependence so we can help each other travel through life, supporting each other with whatever strengths, talents, gifts and abilities he has given to each of us.

The first Christians modeled for us what it means to face the world and travel through life with other believers:

> And all the believers met together in one place and shared everything they had. They sold their property and possessions and shared the money with those in need. They worshiped together at the Temple each day, met in homes for the Lord's Supper, and shared their meals with great joy and generosity—all the while praising God and enjoying the goodwill of all the people. And each

day the Lord added to their fellowship those who were being saved. (Acts 2:44–47)

Redefining body

Growing up Catholic I learned that Christ's body is present in the host we receive at Holy Communion. Early in my faith journey as an adult, when I participated in Communion in various Protestant churches I heard "This is the body of Christ shed for you" as the bread was held up. This perpetuated my belief that Christ's body on earth is indeed present in the host or the bread one receives at Communion. As I grew in my faith, I gradually came to understand that Christ's body on earth is not the Communion host or bread. The host or the bread is merely a representation or reminder of what Jesus did by allowing his body to be broken for us. I learned that Christ's body on earth is any group of believers who come together to follow Jesus and walk the Christian walk—in other words, a church. If you had asked 1st-century Christians what a church was or why you should go to church, they would not have understood the question. Why? Because they *were* the church.

Important decisions

The most important decision anyone will ever make, I believe, is whether or not to be a child of God, a member of God's family. This decision not only determines where one will spend eternity; it also determines the quality of one's life while on earth. Make no mistake, this decision needs to be conscious and intentional. To not decide is, in essence, to keep yourself apart from God's family.

The second most important decision one will ever make, I believe, is deciding which church body to be part of. If one decides to become a child of God, the church family where one plants oneself is a critical determining factor in how one will grow as a Christian. I encourage you to also make this decision a conscious and intentional one—i.e., don't base your decision on location or on what denomination you grew up in, if you grew up in a church. I encourage you to look carefully at a prospective church body to see if it is a healthy, new covenant church. More on this in a bit.

A vision for the Church

Bill Hybels, founding pastor of Willow Creek Community Church near Chicago, possesses a vision for the church and a profound belief in the power of the church that can only be God-given. His passion for what churches can be and are meant to be exudes from the pages of his book *Courageous Leadership*. He states, "The local church is the hope of the world."[37] He goes on to explain this by saying

> There is nothing like the local church when it's working right. Its beauty is indescribable. Its power is breathtaking. Its potential is unlimited. It comforts the grieving and heals the broken in the context of community. It builds bridges to seekers and offers truth to the confused. It provides resources for those in need and opens its arms to the forgotten, the downtrodden, the disillusioned. It breaks the chains of addictions,

frees the oppressed, and offers belonging to the marginalized of this world. Whatever the capacity for human suffering, the church has a greater capacity for healing and wholeness. Still to this day, the potential of the local church is almost more than I can grasp. No other organization on earth is like the church. Nothing even comes close.[38]

When I first read those words I couldn't help but wonder why so many churches aren't working right. If this is what churches are meant to be, and indeed can be, why is it that so many churches are not like this? As I pondered this question the answer that came to my mind was this: many churches are not like this because they function according to the old covenant rather the new covenant, and because they are not healthy.

Old covenant churches versus new covenant churches

New covenant churches believe in and follow the teachings of Jesus (salvation by faith). Old covenant churches believe in and follow the Law of Moses (salvation by works). New covenant churches teach relationship. Old covenant churches teach religion. New covenant churches focus on the heart. Old covenant churches focus on behavior. New covenant churches are led by spiritual leaders. Old covenant churches are led by religious leaders. New covenant churches are inclusive. Old covenant churches are exclusive.

To illustrate the difference between an old covenant church and a new covenant church, take a look at an event that occurred during Jesus's earthly ministry:

One Sabbath day as Jesus was teaching in a synagogue, he saw a woman who had been crippled by an evil spirit. She had been bent double for eighteen years and was unable to stand up straight. When Jesus saw her, he called her over and said, "Dear woman, you are healed of your sickness!" Then he touched her, and instantly she could stand straight. How she praised God!

But the leader in charge of the synagogue was indignant that Jesus had healed her on the Sabbath day. "There are six days of the week for working," he said to the crowd. "Come on those days to be healed, not on the Sabbath."

But the Lord replied, "You hypocrites! Each of you works on the Sabbath day! Don't you untie your ox or your donkey from its stall on the Sabbath and lead it out for water? This dear woman, a daughter of Abraham, has been held in bondage by Satan for eighteen years. Isn't it right that she be released, even on the Sabbath?" (Luke 13:10–16)

If this were to happen in today's world, an old covenant church would be upset that the rules were being broken. A new covenant church would celebrate the healing.

Heart versus behavior

As I made the transition from religion to relationship I gradually came to understand that God is a God of hearts. He is not nearly as interested in what I do as in why I do it. I realized that God doesn't want us to give him our behavior; he wants us to give him our hearts. "'Turn your hearts to the LORD, the God of Israel'" (Joshua 24:23). I learned that he is not interested in right behavior if it is fueled by wrong motives, and that right behavior flows from a right heart, not vice versa. "'A good person produces good things from the treasury of a good heart, and an evil person produces evil things from the treasury of an evil heart'" (Matthew 12:35).

As God performed surgery on my heart to align it with his values, I began to see that I needed to put him front and center in my life and make my relationship with him my top priority. That was the only way my heart would be right. As I did this I came to understand that religion can be practiced in one's spare time; however, relationship requires total commitment. "Don't look for shortcuts to God. The market is flooded with surefire, easygoing formulas for a successful life that can be practiced in your spare time. Don't fall for that stuff, even though crowds of people do. The way to life—to God! —is vigorous and requires total attention" (Matthew 7:13–14 MSG).

Spiritual leaders versus religious leaders

When I first started to walk with Jesus I did not understand the difference between being religious and being spiritual. Joyce Meyer helped me to understand this difference in her teaching series "Religion or Relationship?" In that teaching she defined religion as "man's ideas of God's expectations" and went on to say, "Religion is rules & regulations. It's all the things you have to do to be acceptable to God." She also stated that religious people "do works for the wrong reasons, not out of relationship," while spiritual people are "responsive to and controlled by the Holy Spirit."[39] The apostle Paul made this same point to the church in Galatia when he said, "When you are directed by the Spirit, you are not under obligation to the law of Moses" (Galatians 5:18). Therefore, if a church body is to truly operate according to the new covenant, it needs to be led by someone who is spiritual, not someone who is religious.

Important Note: It would be a mistake to assume that because someone holds a leadership position in a church he or she is a spiritual leader. I'm afraid there are many churches that are being led by religious leaders or, worse, secular leaders who have somehow attained the title of pastor.

Henry and Richard Blackaby, in their book *Spiritual Leadership*, make a number of important points regarding spiritual leaders and spiritual leadership. These points are:

1. Spiritual leadership is not an occupation; it is a calling. Spiritual leadership . . . is not a role for which one applies. Rather, it is assigned by God.[40]

2. Spiritual leaders understand that God is their leader. . . . Spiritual leaders are directed by the Holy Spirit, not by their own agendas. . . . Spiritual leaders do not try to satisfy the goals and ambitions of the people they lead but those of the God they serve.[41]

3. Without the Spirit's presence, people may be leaders, but they are not spiritual leaders.... Unless God sets the agenda for a leader's life, that person, though thoroughly educated, will not be an effective spiritual leader.[42]

4. Leaders seek to move people on to God's agenda, all the while being aware that only the Holy Spirit can ultimately accomplish the task.[43]

5. The primary goal of spiritual leadership ... is taking people from where they are to where God wants them to be.[44]

6. Spiritual leaders must bring followers into a face-to-face encounter with God so they hear from God directly, not indirectly through their leader.... The key to spiritual leadership, then, is to encourage followers to grow in their relationship with their Lord.[45]

Throughout my faith journey I have been led by many church leaders. Some have been spiritual leaders, and some have been religious leaders. As I look back and reflect, I can distinguish between the two types of leaders by how I felt when I was around them. When I was being led by spiritual leaders, I felt relaxed and accepted for who I was. I could verbalize questions and doubts freely, knowing that someone would be there to help me sort it out and find answers. I could take deep breaths in and out, and I could stretch my muscles. When I was being led by religious leaders, on the other hand, I felt uncomfortable, guarded, defensive and not good enough. My breathing was constricted, and my muscles were tight. I was afraid to say out loud what I was thinking, for I was fairly sure I would encounter judgment rather than understanding.

Ordination versus anointing

When God assigns someone to be a spiritual leader, he anoints that person for leadership. This is very different from someone deciding to go into professional ministry and being given the seal of approval—that is, ordained—by human beings to do that work. Wikipedia defines ordination as "the process by which individuals are consecrated, that is, set apart as clergy to perform various religious rites and ceremonies." Inherent in this definition is the understanding that it is human beings who are doing the consecrating.

The difference between ordination and anointing is that God is at the center of the anointing process, and human beings are at the center of the ordination process. In the *Maxwell Leadership Bible* John Maxwell defines anointing as "God's intimate presence and enabling power."[46]

It is important to understand that someone can be ordained by human beings to do something and not be anointed by God to do that same thing. It is also possible that someone can be anointed by God to do something and not have the approval or blessing of human beings to do it. As it is sometimes difficult to discern whether someone is anointed or simply ordained, here are some indicators that may be helpful in the discerning process.

According to John Maxwell, "Anointed leadership is characterized by:

1. Charisma—the anointed enjoy a sense of giftedness that comes from God. It seems magnetic.

2. Character—people see God's nature in his or her leadership. They trust the individual.

3. Competence—the leader has the ability to get the job done. His or her leadership produces results.

4. Conviction—the leader has backbone. He or she always stands for what is right.[47]

Additional indicators that point to a divine anointing are determination, focus, internal motivation, contagious passion and an all-consuming vision.

The determination of someone who is anointed by God to lead is an absolute refusal to give up. Joyce Meyer describes this as a "holy determination" to "press on until we see the fulfillment of God's plan for our life."[48]

Internal motivation can also be described as self-discipline. Someone who is internally motivated does not need anyone else to tell them what to do or when to do it. The impetus for action comes from inside them. It comes from the vision God has given them for their life and the passion that vision evokes in them.

Bill Hybels discusses passion and vision in his book *Courageous Leadership*. He states, "Vision and passion are inextricably bound together in the life of a leader." He defines vision as a "picture of the future that produces passion" and says, "Vision is the fuel that leaders run on. It's the energy that creates action. It's the fire that ignites the passion of followers."[49]

Before moving on from this section there is one important point I would like to highlight. That is, it is important to remember that though someone may be anointed by God that individual is still human and, therefore, not perfect. He or she will make mistakes and will have flaws. The mistakes and the flaws do not cancel out the divine anointing, and the divine anointing does not remove all traces of an imperfect human nature.

Inclusive versus exclusive

Bruxy Cavey discusses the inclusive/exclusive dynamic in his book *The End of Religion*:

> When faith becomes religion, people on the inside of the group begin to focus their attention on the perimeter, patrolling the boundaries to regulate who is in and who is out. They develop visible boundary markers, demarcations of holiness, which become important signs of group identity... Groups that focus on their center may have less clear perimeters. But they will not be threatened by this perimeter ambiguity, because they are clear about the core of their identity. This, in turn, leads to greater compassion and acceptance . . . Jesus-followers will not try to

separate who is "saved" and who is not, who is in and who is out. Policing the perimeter is what religious people do, but not Christ-followers— at least, not Christ-followers who really want to follow Jesus.[50]

Healthy bodies

Any body, if it is to function properly and fulfill the purpose for which it was created, needs to be healthy. The body of Christ is no exception. If a local church is to be effective at continuing Christ's work in the world, it needs to be healthy.

Note: Families tend to be classified as either functional (healthy) or dysfunctional (unhealthy). In reality, no family is one-hundred percent functional or one-hundred percent dysfunctional. Every family has functional characteristics and dysfunctional characteristics. It is a continuum, and each family falls somewhere on the continuum between functional and dysfunctional. In my opinion, the same holds true for church families. For the purpose of this discussion, church families will be referred to as functional or healthy if they have more functional characteristics than dysfunctional ones, and vice versa for dysfunctional or unhealthy.

Characteristics of a healthy (functional) church family:

1. Open communication is encouraged. Members feel free to talk about anything.

2. The structure and operating principles are not taken from a denominational blueprint.

They are designed to fit the needs of that particular congregation and to aid that congregation in fulfilling its specific, God-given purpose.

3. Members feel both accepted for who they are at present and supported to become who God created them to be.

My experience as a family therapist convinced me that any organization or system is only as healthy as its leaders. I saw this evidenced countless times with families. If the parents, the leaders of the family, were sick or dysfunctional, the whole family was sick or dysfunctional. When a parent or parents brought a child in for therapy, claiming the child was the problem in the family, I didn't have to look long or hard to find the dysfunction in the parent or parents. As a result of these experiences, I have an unshakable belief that the marital relationship is the most important relationship in the family. It is the foundation of the family. The health of this relationship determines the health of the family. In order for this relationship to be fully functional, the mother needs to have a healthy relationship with herself, God, and the father, and the father needs to have a healthy relationship with himself, God, and the mother. If this is the case, the family is likely healthy, and the children have a better than average chance to be functional. If the opposite is true, the children will likely be stressed and will adapt in dysfunctional ways.

The same holds true for church families. I firmly believe that the relationships among the leaders of a congregation are the most important human relationships in a church. If the leaders of a particular church body or church family are sick or dysfunctional, the body will be contaminated, and the church family will likely be unhealthy. If the leaders are healthy and functional, the body will likely be healthy, and the church will have a better than average chance of bringing people into relationship with Jesus and helping them grow into mature Christians.

In my opinion the health of leaders in a church family can be measured according to the same criteria as the health of parents in a biological family—that is, each leader needs to have relationships with God, self and the other leaders of that congregation that are marked by love, trust, respect and acceptance. When this is not the case, agendas other than God's tend to take center stage.

What to look for

In order to determine whether a particular church body or congregation is a healthy, new covenant church, one needs to look at a number of factors. First and foremost, Jesus needs to be the head of the body, the foundation of the church. Next, the human head of the church body, the senior pastor, needs to be spiritually mature, and those representing the next level of leadership, paid staff and lay leaders, need to be healthy and unified.

In a biological family the major task of the parents is to provide for the needs of each other and the children. This enables each family member to develop into an individual who is healthy physically, mentally, emotionally and spiritually. It is no different in church families. The major task of church leaders is to provide for the needs of each other and the congregation so that individual members can grow into people who are spiritually healthy and mature, and the church body as a whole can be healthy and mature. If the church body is not healthy, it is doubtful that this body will be able to effectively carry out Jesus' work in the world.

Personal Note: I did not consider any of these factors when I first started to travel in church circles as an adult. It never entered my mind that I needed to think about whether the church I was attending was healthy or unhealthy, whether the leaders were committed to serving God or to fulfilling personal agendas, and whether or not they were truly preaching the good news of Jesus Christ— that is, the new covenant. I naively assumed that church bodies and church leaders were committed to serving God and operating with integrity. This false assumption and my failure to consider the above factors led to my being deeply wounded by church leaders when I tried to grow into the person God had created me to be and to fulfill the purpose he had chosen for me and created me to fulfill.

CHAPTER ELEVEN

DISCIPLES

Once an individual accepts God's invitation for relationship and becomes part of his family, that individual needs to decide whether or not to become a disciple of Jesus. As with any relationship, there are varying degrees of closeness and commitment that are possible. We can be as close to God or as distant from him as we choose to be—for example, casual acquaintance, friend, best friend, or disciple.

A disciple is one who is taught. Marcus J. Borg, in his book *Jesus A New Vision*, discusses what it means to be a disciple of Jesus Christ. Borg states, "To be a disciple of Jesus meant something more than being a student of a teacher. To be a disciple meant 'to follow after.' 'Whoever would be my disciple.' Jesus said, 'Let him follow me.' What does it mean to be a follower of Jesus? It means to take seriously what he took seriously, to be like him in some sense."[51]

As stated in chapter six, when Jesus walked the earth in the flesh he consistently taught that love is more important than the law. He also consistently manifested compassion for anyone who was hurting or struggling. Therefore, it seems blatantly clear that Jesus took loving people seriously. During the last meal he shared with the twelve apostles before he died, he told them, "I am giving you a new commandment: Love each other. Just as I have loved you, you should love each other. Your love for one another will prove to the world that you are my disciples" (John 13:34–35).

That command was not only for the apostles who knew Jesus in the flesh; it was and is for all his disciples throughout time. The love that followers of Jesus are called to exhibit, though, is not a worldly love. It is a Calvary-type love. What is a Calvary-type love? It is a verb. It is a choice. It is a selfless love. It is choosing to do something for someone else regardless of the cost to self. It is not a feeling. It is an action. It is Jesus carrying his cross to Calvary in Jerusalem and allowing Roman soldiers to nail him to it, and then staying nailed to it until he died.

Calvary-type love

Gregory Boyd, in his book *Repenting of Religion*, provides a description of Calvary-type love:

> While nonbelievers can be expected to love those who love them, disciples are called and empowered to love even their enemies and pray for those who persecute them. While nonbelievers can be expected to do good to those who do good to them, disciples are called and empowered to do good even to those who harm them . . . Our love must be given without consideration to the relative merits or faults of the person we encounter . . . We are to love without

strings attached, without conditions, without any consideration whatsoever of the apparent worthiness of the person we encounter.[52]

Bruxy Cavey, in his book *The End of Religion*, provides another description of Calvary-type love:

The way of Jesus is the way of risky love. Religion is the way of safety, security and shelter within the structure of rules, regulations, rituals, and routines. Jesus and his earliest followers were relentless in pressing people to see two things. First, loving people is the primary way we love God. Second, this love of humankind must always take precedence over religious ritual or ethnic obstacles ... Christ-followers are called to be, according to the standards of this world, "foolish." Real love is, from a purely human, self-serving perspective, irrational ... Religious traditions can be a trap that keeps us from moving into unchartered territories of bold love and radical compassion. Irreligious people, on the other hand, are free to be more loving. Jesus calls people to love in such a way that all social barricades are broken, penetrated, subverted—including and especially those erected by religion. And to love like God wants, we must be willing to put practical service ahead of safety, comfort and convenience.[53]

Needless to say, loving others with a Calvary-type love is far from easy. So what does it take to love like this? It takes first allowing oneself to be loved unconditionally. It is through the experience of being loved that one develops a healthy self-love. If you don't have love for self, you can't give love to others. Jesus himself made this point when he answered a question posed to him by a teacher of religious law: "'Which is the most important command . . . ?' Jesus replied, 'Love the Lord your God with all your heart, soul, and mind. This is the first and greatest commandment. The second most important is similar: Love your neighbor as much as you love yourself'" (Matthew 22:36–39 TLB). The operative words here are "as much as you love yourself." Again, if you don't have love for self, you can't give love to others. You can't give away what you don't have.

Bruxy Cavey put it this way: "Real Christ-followers are those who, having been on the receiving end of God's gracious love through Jesus, pour out this same embracing love to others in ways that mend broken relationships, heal inner wounds, and offer practical care for the helpless and hurting."[54]

Keeping oneself fueled

In order to consistently love with a Calvary-type love, one needs to be running on a full tank. Running on empty won't cut it. Refueling happens through the sun and water of our relationship with God—prayer and worship.

When I think about a follower of Jesus Christ, the image that comes to my mind is someone who has a retractable roof on the top of their head. Through prayer and worship that roof can be opened at any time, and life-giving, unconditional love and grace and power can flow through them, filling every nook, cranny and crevice of their being. Once full, their arms stretch out in front of them, and that same love and grace and power flow out of each of their ten fingers to anyone and everyone they come in contact with. Sounds wonderful, doesn't it? I can assure you from personal experience that it is wonderful. Allowing oneself to be loved by God and then allowing oneself to be used by God to love others is one of the payoffs of becoming a disciple.

Something else

In addition to commanding us to love one another, Jesus told us what else we need to do if we wish to be his disciple: "If you do not carry your own cross and follow me, you cannot be my disciple" (Luke 14:27).

Carrying your cross means being obedient to God, fulfilling the purpose he chose especially for you. Jesus came to earth to die on a cross. That was his purpose. God also put each of us on earth to fulfill a specific purpose that he chose for us and designed us to fulfill. Whether or not we fulfill it—that is, carry our cross—is up to us. It is our choice. It is in carrying that cross, however, that we become fully who God created us to be. When we become who God created us to be and do what God created us to do, we experience an internal joy and sense of fulfillment that is beyond human understanding or attainment. It is something that can come only from God.

If you are not sure whether you believe that God has a specific purpose for each individual he creates, consider the fact that the concept of God having a plan and a purpose for every individual he creates is referenced in both the Old and the New Testaments.

Isaiah told Cyrus, a pagan king, that God wanted him
to facilitate the release of the people of Judah from exile
in Babylon so they could return to Jerusalem and rebuild
the temple. When the people questioned God for working
through a pagan king, Isaiah told them,

> "What sorrow awaits those who argue with their
> Creator.
>> Does a clay pot argue with its maker?
> Does the clay dispute with the one who shapes
> it, saying
>> 'Stop, you are doing it wrong!'
> Does the pot exclaim,
>> 'How clumsy can you be!'
> How terrible it would be if a newborn baby said
> to its father,
>> 'Why was I born?
> or if it said to its mother,
>> 'Why did you make me this way?'
> This is what the Lord says —
>> the Holy One of Israel and your Creator:
> 'Do you question what I do for my children?
>> Do you give me orders about the work of
>> my hands?
> I am the one who made the earth
>> and created people to live on it.
> With my hands I stretched out the heavens.
>> All the stars are at my command.
> I will raise up Cyrus to fulfill my righteous purpose,
>> and I will guide his actions.'" (Isaiah 45:9–13)

Isaiah was telling the people of Israel in no uncertain terms that God is sovereign, that he knows what he is doing and that he chooses whomever he wants to do whatever he wants.

Jeremiah also believed that God has a purpose and plan for everyone he creates. Jeremiah relayed this truth in a letter to the Israelites when they were in exile: "'For I know the plans I have for you,' says the LORD. 'They are plans for good and not for disaster, to give you a future and a hope'" (Jeremiah 29:11).

A New Testament figure who believed that God has a specific purpose for each individual he creates, and who had a very clear understanding and acceptance of the role God wanted him to play, was John the Baptist.

> At this time John the Baptist was baptizing at Aenon, near Salim . . . John's disciples came to him and said, "Rabbi, the man you met on the other side of the Jordan River, the one you identified as the Messiah, is also baptizing people. And everybody is going to him instead of coming here to us."
>
> John replied, "No one can receive anything unless God gives it from heaven. You yourselves know how plainly I told you, "I am not the Messiah. I am only here to prepare the way for Him." (John 3:23–28)

The apostle Paul also believed this. In his letter to the church at Corinth, Paul stated, "But we will not boast of authority we do not have. Our goal is to measure up to God's plan for us" (2 Corinthians 10:13 TLB).

Discovering your purpose

If you wish to discover the purpose for which God created you and you don't know how, here are some suggestions:

In *The Purpose Driven Life* Rick Warren gives the following suggestion as to how you might arrive at an understanding of God's purpose for your life:

> Before God created you, he decided what role he wanted you to play on earth. He planned exactly how he wanted you to serve him, and then he shaped you for those tasks. You are the way you are because you were made for a specific ministry . . . God never wastes anything. He would not give you abilities, interests, talents, gifts, personality, and life experiences unless he intended to use them for his glory. By identifying and understanding these factors, you can discover God's will for your life.[55]

> John Maxwell, in *Becoming a Person of Influence*, puts it this way:

> God has created every person with a purpose. But not everyone discovers what that purpose is. To find out, get to know yourself—your strengths and weaknesses. Look at your opportunities. Examine where God has put you.

> Then seek His counsel. He will give you a vision for your life.[56]

The apostle Paul told the church in Rome, and us, that if we want to understand the purpose for which God created us we need to detach from the ways of the world and learn God's ways: "Don't copy the behavior and customs of this world, but let God transform you into a new person by changing the way you think. Then you will learn to know God's will for you, which is good and pleasing and perfect" (Romans 12:2).

The point was made in chapter six that God's standards in no way, shape, or form match the world's standards. Therefore, anyone who is truly living his or her life according to God's standards can't help but stand out to others as belonging to God. Just as God wanted the ancient Israelites to live by a higher standard than their neighbors so their neighbors would know that they were his people, he wants 21st-century Christians to do the same for the same reason.

Bill Hybels, in his book *Too Busy Not to Pray*, describes a genuine disciple of Jesus Christ, an authentic Christian, as follows:

> Authentic Christians are persons who stand apart from others, even other Christians, as though listening to a different drummer. Their character seems deeper, their ideas fresher, their spirit softer, their courage greater, their leadership stronger, their concerns wider, their compassion more genuine, their convictions more concrete. They are joyful in spite of difficult circumstances and show wisdom beyond their years.[57]

Churches as disciples

I believe that just as God has a unique purpose for each individual he creates, he also has a unique purpose for each church body he gives birth to. Henry and Richard Blackaby echo this belief in their book *Spiritual Leadership.* They state, "God equips each church for particular assignments."[58] Before a congregation, or church family, can understand and fulfill its particular assignment, however, it first needs to become, corporately, a genuine disciple of Jesus Christ.

Just as individuals who choose to follow Jesus are called to love with a Calvary-type love, churches that are truly following Jesus (new covenant churches) are also called to love with a Calvary-type love.

How can you tell if a church is truly manifesting Calvary-type love? "When sinful, broken, hurting people are pleasantly surprised at how accepting we are, and religious people are outraged at how accepting we are, there is a good chance we're starting to live like Jesus."[59]

Important Note: Acceptance is not the same as agreement. We can accept people for who they are and love them for who they are without agreeing with or condoning what they do. We are called to love, not to judge. Jesus told us this in his Sermon on the Mount: "Do not judge others, and you will not be judged" (Matthew 7:1).

Gregory Boyd put it this way:

Sin ruptured the fellowship and sidetracked the plan. It was restored in Christ, however, and the purpose of the church now is to re-express the original goal of creation by living it before the world . . . the church as a whole has repeatedly failed to fulfill this mandate . . . We have tended to define ourselves as the promoter of good against evil and have often seen ourselves as specialists on good and evil. We have consequently become judges of good and evil rather than lovers of people regardless of whether they are good or evil . . . All are supposed to see God as his love is displayed in the Body of Christ. Through the church, the world is supposed to literally witness and experience the perfect love that God eternally is. If the hearts of those in the world are at all open, they acknowledge the reality of the triune God because he is right there in front of them—in the loving community of the church!

They witness firsthand the reality of Jesus because they encounter "his body."[60]

Further, if a particular church body is truly a disciple of Jesus Christ it ministers to people in the same ways that Jesus ministered to people when he walked the earth in the flesh. The point was made in the previous chapter that Jesus meant for the church to be his hands, feet and heart in the world after his physical body died. He intended for his followers to continue ministering to people as he had. Since healing and teaching were the two primary aspects of Jesus' earthly ministry, it would seem to logically follow that the two primary functions of a church should be the same—healing and teaching.

Healing ministry

I can't imagine I would get much of an argument from anyone when I say that the world is full of hurting, broken people who are struggling with anxiety, depression, anger management, addictions to all kinds of substances and behaviors, and on and on and on. Though there are many services and programs that help with all these struggles, many only deal with the visible manifestations of these problems. The roots of the problems, the reasons the struggles exist in the first place, are often overlooked. It has been my experience that the only thing that can truly heal the roots of the problems individuals struggle with is Jesus' love.

Broken, hurting, struggling people sought out Jesus. The Bible is full of stories of people who flocked to him, followed him, chased him down, overcame obstacles to get to him. Why? They knew he loved them, they knew he could heal them, and they felt safe enough to go to him. As members of his body, the church, we need to be conveying the same love, hope and safety through creating an environment that is devoid of judgment and exhibiting Calvary-type love.

Gregory Boyd puts it this way: "The community in which performance and hiding have ceased is a community in which healing can occur . . . Emotional wounds that are concealed are wounds that can never be healed. Only when people feel safe enough to reveal their innermost pain are they able to begin to deal with it, but this sort of safety requires a context that is free of judgment."[61]

As Bill Hybels states:

One major facet of the beauty of the local church is its power to transform the human heart . . . Only one power exists on this sorry planet that can do that. It's the power of the love of Jesus

Christ, the love that conquers sin and wipes out shame and heals wounds and reconciles enemies and patches broken dreams and ultimately changes the world, one life at a time. And what grips my heart every day is the knowledge that the radical message of that transforming love has been given to the church. . . . In a very real way the future of the world rests in the hands of local congregations.[62]

In my opinion, the only way a local congregation can effectively communicate to the world the radical message of Christ's transforming love is to teach and live the true gospel, i.e., lay their own hurts and struggles at the feet of Jesus, allow him to heal them, tell others how Jesus healed them and continually point others toward Jesus for their healing.

Teaching ministry

The authors of *Breaking the Bondage of Legalism* state, "Millions of Americans who truly are Christian have failed to fully comprehend the gospel. It is as if they have one foot in the new covenant and another in the old."[63] When this happens, when regular churchgoers do not have a clear understanding of the true gospel, it breaks my heart, and I hold the leaders and teachers of their churches accountable for this. I believe that if regular churchgoers do not understand the gospel it is most probably because they are not being taught the true gospel. The gospel is not complicated. It can be boiled down to:

1. Salvation is through faith in Jesus Christ. Period. There is nothing we can do to earn salvation.

2. When we accept Jesus' work on the cross as a personal gift, repent of our wrongdoings and give our lives to him, we come into relationship with God, becoming part of his family.

3. The Holy Spirit then takes up residence inside us and slowly but surely transforms us from the inside out until we become like Jesus.

If churches are not teaching this, they are not new covenant churches. If you are not hearing week in and week out how to become part of God's family, how to nurture your relationship with God, how to hear from him and how to become more like Jesus, you will have an uphill struggle to become who God wants you to be, and you may never experience the freedom that is available to you in Christ. I agree wholeheartedly with Bruxy Cavey when he says, "The real problem Christians need to face is not the exaggerated criticism of secular people, but the mind-blowing extent of the church's failure to follow Jesus."[64]

Not of this world

Just as Jesus' followers are to be in the world but not of the world, his church is to be in the world but not of the world. When Jesus stood before the Roman governor, Pontius Pilate, Pilate asked him, "Are you the king of the

Jews?" (John 18:33). Jesus answered, "My Kingdom is not an earthly kingdom. . . . My Kingdom is not of this world" (John 18:36).

In his Sermon on the Mount Jesus told his followers to be light in a dark world. "'You are the light of the world—like a city on a hilltop that cannot be hidden. No one lights a lamp and then puts it under a basket. Instead, a lamp is placed on a stand, where it gives light to everyone in the house. In the same way, let your good deeds shine out for all to see, so that everyone will praise your heavenly Father'" (Matthew 5:14–16). I believe that Jesus wants the same thing from his church that he wants from his individual followers—i.e., to be light in a dark world. If his church is indeed to be light in a dark world, then the church most definitely needs to be so different from the world it is in that it stands out brightly and draws people to it.

The point was made earlier that God's standards in no way, shape or form match those of the world. An authentic Christian has been described as someone who marches to the beat of a different drummer. Following this same line of thinking, a healthy, new covenant church would be one that operates according to standards that in no way, shape or form match those of the world and that marches to the beat of a different drummer. This church would not gauge its success or failure by the standards of the world (money, numbers, size). Rather, the measuring stick of success or failure for this church would be God's standard. What is God's standard? What does God want from us? As stated previously, God wants us to love people, to obey him and to fulfill the purpose for which we were created. It would seem to logically follow that in order for a particular church body to be successful in God's eyes it needs to do the same.

The stakes are high

"Without churches so filled with the power of God that they can't help but spill goodness and peace and love and joy into the world, depravity will win the day; evil will flood the world. But it doesn't have to be that way. Strong, growing communities of faith can turn the tide of history."[65]

In my opinion "strong, growing communities of faith" are healthy, new covenant churches that are led by courageous spiritual leaders who fully embrace and live out "the great irony."

> So here is the great irony—Jesus is happy to see his followers get organized in order to help spread the message that organizations are not the answer. Christ-followers read the Bible to learn of Jesus' teaching that reading the Bible is not what makes us a Christian. We pray regularly in order to commune with the God who reminds us that praying regularly is not what makes us acceptable to him. We meditate to immerse our souls in the love of God that is already ours, not in order to somehow achieve a state of self-induced enlightenment. And we go to church to collectively celebrate the message that going to church is not what makes us God's children.[66]

CHAPTER TWELVE

ENOUGH

As you read in the introduction, I grew into a compulsive overachiever and compulsive caretaker at a young age. I did this because I believed that I needed to earn self-worth and love by pleasing people and gaining their approval. I had to always be "doing"; just "being" was out of the question. Chronic feelings of inadequacy and anxiety accompanied these behaviors because it seemed to me that no matter what I did, how much I did or how well I did it, it was never enough. The faulty belief that was underneath all of this, in addition to the belief that I was not lovable for just "being," was an unrealistic definition of "enough." My picture of *enough* was totally beyond what any human being could possibly accomplish. Therefore, the feelings of inadequacy and anxiety never left me.

As you read at the end of chapter one, when I began my career as a mental health professional I learned that it was toxic shame that had fueled the dysfunction in my family of origin and was fueling my compulsive and performance-based behaviors.

As you read in chapters three, four and eight, I began a healing process for my emotional and spiritual wounds in my early adulthood. This healing process lasted several decades and involved walking several different paths, each of which contributed significant pieces to the healing. The most significant pieces came through working the Christ-centered 12 Steps in Celebrate Recovery. This is when the toxic shame was finally healed. I learned that my worth and value come solely from being a child of God. I belong to him and know that he will never abandon me or forsake me. I don't have to please others or gain others' approval in order for God to love me. He loves me no matter what, and he knew me and loved me before he placed me in my mother's womb. There is nothing I can do to make him love me, and there is nothing I can do to make him not love me. Feeling secure in his love I can now gratefully live my life for him. I am no longer bound by a sick need to please human beings and obtain their approval. I am living my life for an audience of One.

Even though my toxic shame was healed and I finally felt comfortable in my own skin, something was still missing. It still wasn't quite enough. It became enough when I picked up my cross and began to carry it. "'If you do not carry your own cross and follow me, you cannot be my disciple'" (Luke 14:27). Contrary to popular opinion, carrying our cross does not result in pain and suffering. Rather, "in carrying that cross, we find liberty and joy and fulfillment."[67]

Finding which cross to pick up was not quick or easy. Carrying the cross was even harder, though the difficulties and pain of carrying the cross were balanced by a deep feeling of certainty (I knew that I knew that I knew) that I was exactly where I was supposed to be, doing exactly what I was created to do. The peace that accompanied this was the peace that surpasses human understanding, the peace that can come only from God. Nothing else can compare to the peace and the joy you experience when you are walking in the will of God for your life, when you know you are right where you are supposed to be, doing exactly what you were created to do, fulfilling God's purpose for your life. And it all begins with accepting the gift he sent us at Christmas: his Son, Jesus Christ.

I would like to end this book by sharing the story of how I found the cross that had my name on it, and what the experience of carrying it has been like.

Carrying my cross

Fairly early in my faith walk (mid- to late 1990s) I started experiencing a nagging sense that I was supposed to do something for God. It kept gnawing at me inside and wouldn't go away. Though I had this feeling that I was supposed to do something for God, I didn't have the faintest idea what it was I was supposed to do. In an effort to try to understand what I was supposed to do, I served on and then led a committee in my church and also served in a number of different ministries. Though these were good and enjoyable and somewhat fulfilling, not one of them felt like the right fit.

In 2003 I was leading a group in the church's small group ministry. In spring/early summer of that year a notice went out to all the small group leaders that the senior pastor was going to Saddleback Church in California to learn about a faith-based recovery program called Celebrate Recovery. The notice included an open invitation for anyone who was interested to join him. I went, and while I was there God finally let me know what he wanted me to do for him.

The last day of the summit I went to a workshop titled "Women Can Be CR Leaders Too," led by Tonya Roberts, a CR ministry leader in Florida. I thought that workshop was going to be about women in any leadership role in CR. Within the first five minutes, however, Tonya made it clear that she was specifically talking about the role of the ministry leader who oversees the entire ministry. Tonya then began to list and talk about the spiritual gifts and personality characteristics a CR ministry leader needs to have in order to be effective and successful. As she listed them I realized that every gift and personality characteristic she listed, I possessed.

It slowly started dawning on me that I was supposed to lead the ministry. That was quite an unsettling thought, as I was fairly sure none of the other eight people from my church who were at the summit were even remotely thinking of me as the leader. In addition, I was beginning to have a glimmer of understanding of what a huge responsibility and commitment this would involve.

When we got home the church did decide to start a Celebrate Recovery ministry, and I did become the ministry leader. Now, one would think that once you understand what God's purpose for your life is and you begin to live that purpose, it would be smooth sailing. Nothing could be further from the truth. The year that followed was one of the most difficult, if not *the* most difficult, year of my life. Establishing and leading the Celebrate Recovery ministry was far harder than I had ever imagined it would be. It was full of struggle, challenges, conflict, anger, hurt, fear and self-doubt. Power battles abounded. My leadership was constantly challenged and undermined. There was a period of time in spring '04 during which I was particularly discouraged and full of doubt. One morning while I was praying I asked God to show me what I needed to read or to hear, and I opened my Bible. It opened to 1 Chronicles 28 (David commissioning Solomon to build the temple). I started to read that chapter, and the last two verses almost jumped off the page at me: "Then David continued, 'Be strong and courageous and do the work. Don't be afraid or discouraged, for the LORD God, my God, is with you. He will not fail you or forsake you. He will see to it that all the work related to the Temple of the LORD is finished correctly. The various divisions of priests and Levites will serve in the Temple of God. Others with skills of every kind will volunteer, and the officials and the entire nation are at your command.'"

This confirmed to me that God did indeed want me to be a leader. I began to read those verses every day, sometimes multiple times in one day, and I slowly began to feel the burden of weight lifted off my shoulders. I *knew* that I wasn't alone and that God was in control. I didn't have to be. All I had to do was follow his plan and he would do the rest. As I trusted that more and more, my faith became stronger and my fear decreased. I stopped people pleasing and approval seeking and started to truly lead.

In August 2004 I went back to Saddleback Church for the 2004 Celebrate Recovery Summit. The passion and the commitment to Celebrate Recovery emanating from everyone there was tangibly evident. Being there I felt as though I was home. I knew I had finally found the exact right fit. When I returned to my home church and ministry, I began to lead with a greater degree of confidence and purpose. I knew I was walking in the will of God for my life. I knew who God had created me to be, and I not only felt good about it, I rejoiced in it. As I truly led the ministry, the challenges to my leadership and the power struggles intensified. They eventually culminated in a head-on collision with the stained-glass ceiling.

In November '04 I was removed from the position of Celebrate Recovery Ministry Leader by the pastors and some other leaders in the church. I didn't see it coming and was initially in shock. When the shock lessened I was devastated. I began a period of deep grieving and mourning. I was hurt, angry and depressed. I felt as though I was wandering in the wilderness, lost. I've heard it said that great lessons are learned in times of great pain, and that certainly proved to be true for me. It's difficult to describe the depth of joy I had felt at finally discovering and fulfilling God's purpose for my life. It's even more difficult to describe the depth of pain I felt at having that ripped away from me by human beings. Although I was devastated and in more emotional pain than at almost any other time in my life, I never once doubted God's call on my life. I saw my removal from the leadership of Celebrate Recovery as a human thing and not a God thing. At the same time I also believed that it could not have happened unless God had allowed it to happen.

Though God's hand was not the only hand at work in my removal from the leadership of Celebrate Recovery, his hand was mightily at work as I wandered in the wilderness. During this time he taught me many lessons that I desperately needed to learn. He taught me to trust him, his timing and his plan on a much deeper level. He taught me to truly wait on him. "But those who trust in the LORD will find new strength. They will soar high on wings like eagles. They will run and not grow weary. They will walk and not faint" (Isaiah 40:31). God used my time in the wilderness to deepen and strengthen my relationship with him, particularly my dependence on him. He also taught me that my source of self-esteem and self-worth is not in my professional work or in my ministry. It's in my relationship with him and I belong to him, not to any particular church or ministry.

Though God taught me many lessons during my time in the wilderness, the most profound lesson he taught me was how to forgive. My healing process moved along in fits and starts. I experienced victories followed by relapses. As this happened repeatedly, I came to understand that God had a very special purpose for this time in my life.

I gradually began to understand that, just as he had given me the Celebrate Recovery ministry to lead in order to break my spirit of independence, he allowed it to be taken away from me in order to teach me how to forgive. He slowly and convincingly revealed to me my spirit of unforgiveness. I came to see that my life was not characterized by forgiveness, as Jesus wants his followers' lives to be. Rather, my life was characterized by holding grudges and harboring bitterness, resentment and a desire for vengeance. Though I knew that forgiveness is at the heart of the gospel message and had received God's forgiveness for my sins when I accepted Jesus' work on the cross, I was not extending forgiveness to others who had wronged or hurt me. God showed me that I was not walking out this vital part of the Christian walk. He further showed me that my spirit of unforgiveness would stop me from fulfilling my destiny.

As this realization took root in me, I began to study forgiveness. I came across a definition of forgiveness in Lewis B. Smedes's book *The Art of Forgiving*. That definition is: "Forgiving . . . is an art, a practical art, maybe the most neglected of all the healing arts. It is the art of healing inner wounds inflicted by other people's wrongs."[68] As I continued to study forgiveness, I learned what forgiveness is—and what it is not.

I learned that forgiveness is:

- A choice: I don't have to feel like forgiving someone to forgive him.
- A free gift given with no strings attached.
- Surrendering our right to get even.
- Choosing to keep no record of the wrongs
- Being merciful
- Being gracious
- Letting go of bitterness
- A heart condition: Forgiveness takes place in the forgiver's heart. It is intrapersonal, not interpersonal.
- A permanent condition, a lifelong commitment: I cannot forgive someone and take it back later.

I learned that forgiveness is not:

- Forgetting
- Excusing the wrong that was done
- Tolerating the wrong that was done
- Denying the wrong that was done
- Justifying what was done
- Pardoning what was done
- Refusing to take the wrong seriously
- Pretending that we are not hurt
- Erasing the need for consequences
- Quick
- Easy
- A magic balm that takes away feelings of hurt and anger

Though all of the above lessons I learned about forgiveness were important, the three most important ones were:

1. The choice whether or not to forgive does not depend on the wrongdoer's attitude or perception of the wrong. I can choose to forgive someone whether or not they see themselves as having done something wrong and whether or not they are sorry.

2. Forgiveness is not the same thing as reconciliation. I can forgive someone and choose not to re-enter into a relationship with him/her.

3. Forgiveness is an essential, nonnegotiable ingredient in the healing of deep wounds. In these instances, forgiving benefits the forgiver far more than the forgiven.

As I struggled to forgive the pastors and other church leaders who had removed me from the position of Celebrate Recovery Ministry leader, I fought against my desire to get back at them, to make them hurt as much as they had hurt me. During this process I was comforted by the following words of Lewis B. Smedes in *Forgive and Forget: Healing the Hurts We Don't Deserve*: "Nobody seems to be born with much talent for forgiving. We all need to learn from scratch, and the learning almost always runs against the grain."[69]

As I worked on forgiving those who had hurt me, I quickly realized that I could not do it on my own. My desire for vengeance was too strong. I needed God's help, his power. I began to daily ask God to give me an attitude and lifestyle of forgiveness. I simultaneously made a decision that I was no longer going to allow those pastors and leaders to steal my joy. They had already taken too much from me, and I was not going to allow them to take anything more. As I daily prayed this prayer and reiterated my decision, my peace and joy slowly came back, and I was finally able to exit the wilderness.

I eventually found my way to another Celebrate Recovery ministry where I was asked to lead their team. In August 2009 I again attended the Celebrate Recovery Summit at Saddleback Church. The passion and the commitment to Celebrate Recovery emanating from everyone there was the same as it had been five years earlier, and I experienced the same sense of belonging, of being home, that I had previously experienced. God confirmed to me loudly and clearly that he wanted me to be a Celebrate Recovery leader. So I served as the leader of that Celebrate Recovery team for four years.

Those four years were also difficult. Though they were not marked by the same level of conflict, struggle, challenges and power battles as the previous Celebrate Recovery ministry, I did encounter opposition. Most of the opposition I encountered, similar to what Jesus and the early disciples encountered, came from religious people. I was episodically lied about, betrayed, ostracized, abandoned, and had coup attempts organized against me. All of these episodes were orchestrated by religious people. Some were orchestrated by religious leaders. Though these episodes were painful and lonely to live through, not one caused me to doubt the call God had placed on my life. As I looked to God for comfort and strength to get through each episode, my relationship with him deepened, and my resolve to obey him and fulfill the purpose he had chosen for me was strengthened. I drew much comfort from the following words of Jesus in his Sermon on the Mount: "God blesses you when people mock you and persecute you and lie about you and say all sorts of evil things against you because you are my followers. Be happy about it! Be very glad! For a great reward awaits you in heaven. And remember, the ancient prophets were persecuted in the same way" (Matthew 5:11–12).

When 2013 began I started reaping what I had sown and harvesting what I had planted. The consequences of a lifetime of failing to take care of my physical body caught up with me. Some medical problems I had been ignoring could no longer be ignored. I was in need of two major surgeries. I underwent the first surgery in June and scheduled the second surgery for October. In September I stepped out of leadership of the Celebrate Recovery ministry due to feeling as though I was running on empty with no physical, emotional or spiritual resources left inside me to serve in leadership. I spent the following winter healing physically and replenishing spiritually. I also gradually came to realize that my season of being a Celebrate Recovery leader was over. I then entered a period of waiting on God to let me know what he wanted me to do next—and he did.

In July 2014 God lit a fire in my heart to help his daughters be set free from belief systems and practices that reinforce the inequality of the sexes. In response to that fire being lit, I wrote *When Going with the Flow Isn't Enough, Swim Upstream*. I now swim upstream against gender inequality wherever I see it.

Closing thoughts

Following Jesus is not easy, and though there are many rewards, both in our life on earth and in our eternal life to come, those rewards are not always evident. Therefore, during the difficult times, the dark times, I encourage you to remember two things: (1) Jesus covered us in prayer, and (2) he promised to never leave us. Before he died, Jesus prayed for all who would be his disciples throughout time. He prayed, "I am praying not only for these disciples but also for all who will ever believe in me through their message" (John 17:20). When he appeared to the disciples after his resurrection from the dead, he gave them what has come to be called the Great Commission. He said to them: "Go and make disciples of all the nations, baptizing them in the name of the Father and the Son and the Holy Spirit" (Matthew 28:19). He did not leave it at this, though. He did not expect them to accomplish this huge task alone without his help and support. He went on to tell them, "Teach these new disciples to obey all the commands I have given you. And be sure of this: I am with you always, even to the end of the age" (Matthew 28:20).

Whether or not we choose to fulfill our God-anointed purpose—i.e., carry our cross—is up to us. It is our choice. It is in carrying that cross, however, that we become fully who God created us to be. When we become who God created us to be and do what God created us to do, we experience an internal peace and joy that are beyond human understanding or attainment. This is something that can only come from God.

There is another side to this whole concept of fulfilling God's purpose for our life. That is, we are not the only ones who lose when we fail to discover and fulfill our purpose. Due to the system of human interdependence that God designed, everything we do or fail to do affects others. By not discovering and fulfilling God's plan for us, we not only miss out on experiencing joy and peace, but others miss out as well. In *The Purpose Driven Life* Rick Warren states, "God designed each of us so there would be no duplication in the world. No one has the exact same mix of factors that make you unique. That means no one else on earth will ever be able to play the role God planned for you. If you don't make your unique contribution to the body of Christ, it won't be made."[70]

Whether or not individuals and churches fulfill their God-given purposes is no light matter. It is a matter of the utmost importance. The very last thing Jesus said to the apostles, his special disciples, before he ascended into heaven was "Go into all the world and preach the Good News to everyone" (Mark 16:15). This command was not only for his disciples who knew him in the flesh. This command is also for all his disciples (both individuals and churches) throughout time. In whatever particular way he chooses for us to do it, God wants us to tell people about him, to preach the Good News of the forgiveness and salvation that are available to everyone who chooses to believe in and follow his Son.

Don't give up on God because people, including church people, have hurt you. God doesn't want us to trust people; he wants us to trust *him*. Jesus tells us, "Don't let your hearts be troubled. Trust in God, and trust also in me" (John 14:1).

Don't let opposition stop you from doing what you know God wants you to do. The apostle Paul was called by God and anointed to bring the good news of Jesus Christ to the Gentiles, and he endured incredible hardships in fulfilling this calling. "He endured sickness, rejection, and repeated attacks on his life to bring the message of God's forgiveness to needy people. He spoke before Jews, Greeks, and Romans. He defended his faith before kings and emperors. By the end of his life much of the Mediterranean world had been reached with the gospel."[71] Paul himself described the hardships he and his traveling companions endured to do what God had called them to do. These are his words:

> We have been beaten, been put in prison, faced angry mobs, worked to exhaustion, endured sleepless nights, and gone without food. . . . We serve God whether people honor us or despise us, whether they slander us or praise us. We are honest, but they call us imposters.
>
> We are ignored, even though we are well known. We live close to death, but we are still alive. We have been beaten, but we have not been killed. Our hearts ache, but we always have joy. We are poor, but we give spiritual riches to others. We own nothing, and yet we have everything. . . .
>
> Five different times the Jewish leaders gave me thirty-nine lashes. Three times I was beaten with rods. Once I was stoned. Three times I was shipwrecked. Once I spent a whole night and a day adrift at sea. I have traveled on many long journeys. I have faced danger from rivers and from robbers. I have faced danger from my own people, the Jews, as well as from the Gentiles. I have faced danger in the cities, in the deserts, and on the seas. And I have faced danger from men who claim to be believers but are not. I have

worked hard and long, enduring many sleepless nights. I have been hungry and thirsty and have often gone without food. I have shivered in the cold, without enough clothing to keep me warm. (2 Corinthians 6:5, 8–10; 11:24–27)

In spite of all this Paul did not give up. He persevered until he had completed the work God had called him to do. Near the end of his life Paul stated, "I have fought the good fight, I have finished the race, and I have remained faithful (2 Timothy 4:7).

Finally, if you are experiencing difficulty discovering or living your purpose, I encourage you to work a Christ-centered 12-Step recovery program. You very well may have hurts, habits or hang-ups that are impeding you from discovering and/or living your God-anointed purpose. You may believe that you only have to accept Christ as your Lord and Savior for your life to be complete and satisfying. The proclamation that "I am a born again Christian, my past is washed clean, I am a new creature, and Christ has totally changed me" is true. Our Spirits are born again. Our flesh, however, is holding on to a lifetime of hurts, habits and hang-ups. The likelihood that you have no behaviors, thoughts or attitudes that need to be changed and/or wounds that need to be healed is small to nonexistent. I believe that it is impossible for anyone to grow to adulthood without accruing some hurts along the way and developing some destructive habits or hang-ups. To overspiritualize the initial work of salvation may be to deny the actual condition of our lives. Giving our life to God, accepting his free gift of forgiveness and entering into a personal relationship with him is step three. Taking this step assures you that you will spend eternity with him in heaven. You can stop there. Many people do. If you want to live a life of abundance marked by internal peace, joy and fulfillment, however, you need to work the additional nine steps. Working these steps is what improves the quality of your life on earth and increases the possibility of your doing what you were created and shaped to do: making your unique contribution to the body of Christ.

I am going to leave you with some words from the book of Hebrews in the New Testament:

> Since we are surrounded by such a huge crowd of witnesses to the life of faith, let us strip off every weight that slows us down, especially the sin that so easily trips us up. And let us run with endurance the race God has set before us. We do this by keeping our eyes on Jesus, the champion who initiates and perfects our faith. Because of the joy awaiting him, he endured the cross, disregarding its shame. Now he is seated in the place of honor beside God's throne. Think of all the hostility he endured from sinful people; then you won't become weary and give up. (Hebrews 12:1–3)

APPENDIX ONE

The Sermon on the Mount
Matthew 5:1—7:29

One day as he saw the crowds gathering, Jesus went up on the mountainside and sat down. His disciples gathered around him, and he began to teach them.

The Beatitudes

"God blesses those who are poor and realize their
need for him,
> for the Kingdom of Heaven is theirs.
God blesses those who mourn,
> for they will be comforted.
God blesses those who are humble,
> for they will inherit the whole earth.
God blesses those who hunger and thirst for justice,
> for they will be satisfied.
God blesses those who are merciful,
> for they will be shown mercy.

God blesses those whose hearts are pure,
>for they will see God.
God blesses those who work for peace,
>for they will be called the children of God.
God blesses those who are persecuted for doing right,
>for the Kingdom of Heaven is theirs.

"God blesses you when people mock you and persecute you and lie about you and say all sorts of evil things against you because you are my followers. Be happy about it! Be very glad! For a great reward awaits you in heaven. And remember, the ancient prophets were persecuted in the same way.

Teaching about Salt and Light

"You are the salt of the earth. But what good is salt if it has lost its flavor? Can you make it salty again? It will be thrown out and trampled underfoot as worthless.

"You are the light of the world—like a city on a hilltop that cannot be hidden. No one lights a lamp and then puts it under a basket. Instead, a lamp is placed on a stand, where it gives light to everyone in the house. In the same way, let your good deeds shine out for all to see, so that everyone will praise your heavenly Father.

Teaching about the Law

"Don't misunderstand why I have come. I did not come to abolish the law of Moses or the writings of the prophets. No, I came to accomplish their purpose. I tell you the truth, until heaven and earth disappear, not even the smallest detail of God's law will disappear until its purpose is achieved. So if you ignore the least commandment and teach others to do the same, you will be called the least in the Kingdom of Heaven. But anyone who obeys God's laws and teaches them will be called great in the Kingdom of Heaven.

"But I warn you—unless your righteousness is better than the righteousness of the teachers of religious law and the Pharisees, you will never enter the Kingdom of Heaven!

Teaching about Anger

"You have heard that our ancestors were told, 'You must not murder. If you commit murder, you are subject to judgment.' But I say, if you are even angry with someone, you are subject to judgment! If you call someone an idiot, you are in danger of being brought before the court. And if you curse someone, you are in danger of the fires of hell.

"So if you are presenting a sacrifice at the altar in the Temple and you suddenly remember that someone has something against you, leave your sacrifice there at the altar. Go and be reconciled to that person. Then come and offer your sacrifice to God.

"When you are on the way to court with your adversary, settle your differences quickly. Otherwise, your accuser may hand you over to the judge, who will hand you over to an officer, and you will be thrown into prison. And if that happens, you surely won't be free again until you have paid the last penny.

Teaching about Adultery

"You have heard the commandment that says, 'You must not commit adultery.' But I say, anyone who even looks at a woman with lust has already committed adultery with her in his heart. So if your eye—even your good eye—causes you to lust, gouge it out and throw it away. It is better for you to lose one part of your body than for your whole body to be thrown into hell. And if your hand—even your stronger hand—causes you to sin, cut it off and throw it away. It is better for you to lose one part of your body than for your whole body to be thrown into hell.

Teaching about Divorce

"You have heard the law that says, 'A man can divorce his wife by merely giving her a written notice of divorce.' But I say that a man who divorces his wife, unless she has been unfaithful, causes her to commit adultery. And anyone who marries a divorced woman also commits adultery.

Teaching about Vows

"You have also heard that our ancestors were told, 'You must not break your vows; you must carry out the vows you make to the Lord.' But I say, do not make any vows! Do not say, 'By heaven!' because heaven is God's throne. And do not say, 'By the earth!' because the earth is his footstool. And do not say, 'By Jerusalem!' for Jerusalem is the city of the great King. Do not even say, 'By my head!' for you can't turn one hair white or black. Just say a simple, 'Yes, I will,' or 'No, I won't.' Anything beyond this is from the evil one.

Teaching about Revenge

"You have heard the law that says the punishment must match the injury: 'An eye for an eye, and a tooth for a tooth.' But I say, do not resist an evil person! If someone slaps you on the right cheek, offer the other cheek also. If you are sued in court and your shirt is taken from you, give your coat, too. If a soldier demands that you carry his gear for a mile, carry it two miles. Give to those who ask, and don't turn away from those who want to borrow.

Teaching about Love for Enemies

"You have heard the law that says, 'Love your neighbor' and hate your enemy. But I say, love your enemies! Pray for those who persecute you! In that way, you will be acting as true children of your Father in heaven. For he gives his sunlight to both the evil and the good, and he sends rain on the just and the unjust alike. If you love only those who love you, what reward is there for that? Even corrupt tax collectors do that much. If you are kind only to your friends, how are you different than anyone else? Even pagans do that. But you are to be perfect, even as your Father in heaven is perfect.

Teaching about Giving to the Needy

"Watch out! Don't do your good deeds publicly, to be admired by others, for you will lose the reward from your Father in heaven. When you give to someone in need, don't do as the hypocrites do—blowing trumpets in the synagogues and streets to call attention to their acts of charity! I tell you the truth, they have received all the reward they will ever get. But when you give to someone in need, don't let your left hand know what your right hand is doing. Give your gifts in private, and your Father, who sees everything, will reward you.

Teaching about Prayer and Fasting

"When you pray, don't be like the hypocrites who love to pray publicly on street corners and in the synagogues where everyone can see them. I tell you the truth, that is all the reward they will ever get. But when you pray, go away by yourself, shut the door behind you, and pray to your Father in private. Then your Father, who sees everything, will reward you.

"When you pray, don't babble on and on as people of other religions do. They think their prayers are answered merely by repeating their words again and again. Don't be like them, for your Father knows exactly what you need even before you ask him! Pray like this:

Our Father in heaven,
may your name be kept holy.
May your kingdom come soon.
May your will be done on earth,
as it is in heaven.
Give us today the food we need,
and forgive us our sins,
as we have forgiven those who sin against us.
And don't let us yield to temptation,
but rescue us from the evil one.

"If you forgive those who sin against you, your heavenly Father will forgive you. But if you refuse to forgive others, your Father will not forgive your sins.

"And when you fast, don't make it obvious, as the hypocrites do, for they try to look miserable and disheveled so people will admire them for their fasting. I tell you the truth, that is the only reward they will ever get. But when you fast, comb your hair and wash your face. Then no one will notice that you are fasting, except your Father, who knows what you do in private. And your Father, who sees everything, will reward you.

Teaching about Money and Possessions

"Don't store up treasures here on earth, where moths eat them and rust destroys them, and where thieves break in and steal. Store your treasures in heaven, where moths and rust cannot destroy, and thieves do not break in and steal. Wherever your treasure is, there the desires of your heart will also be.

"Your eye is a lamp that provides light for your body. When your eye is good, your whole body is filled with light. But when your eye is bad, your whole body is filled with darkness. And if the light you think you have is actually darkness, how deep that darkness is!

"No one can serve two masters. For you will hate one and love the other; you will be devoted to one and despise the other. You cannot serve God and be enslaved to money.

"That is why I tell you not to worry about everyday life—whether you have enough food and drink, or enough clothes to wear. Isn't life more than food, and your body more than clothing? Look at the birds. They don't plant or harvest or store food in barns, for your heavenly Father feeds them. And aren't you far more valuable to him than they are? Can all your worries add a single moment to your life?

"And why worry about your clothing? Look at the lilies of the field and how they grow. They don't work or make their clothing, yet Solomon in all his glory was not dressed as beautifully as they are. And if God cares so wonderfully for wildflowers that are here today and thrown into the fire tomorrow, he will certainly care for you. Why do you have so little faith?

"So don't worry about these things, saying, 'What will we eat? What will we drink? What will we wear?' These things dominate the thoughts of unbelievers, but your heavenly Father already knows all your needs. Seek the Kingdom of God above all else, and live righteously, and he will give you everything you need.

"So don't worry about tomorrow, for tomorrow will bring its own worries. Today's trouble is enough for today.

Do Not Judge Others

"Do not judge others, and you will not be judged. For you will be treated as you treat others. The standard you use in judging is the standard by which you will be judged.

"And why worry about a speck in your friend's eye when you have a log in your own? How can you think of saying to your friend, 'Let me help you get rid of that speck in your eye,' when you can't see past the log in your own eye? Hypocrite! First get rid of the log in your own eye; then you will see well enough to deal with the speck in your friend's eye.

"Don't waste what is holy on people who are unholy. Don't throw your pearls to pigs! They will trample the pearls, then turn and attack you.

Effective Prayer

"Keep on asking, and you will receive what you ask for. Keep on seeking, and you will find. Keep on knocking, and the door will be opened to you. For everyone who asks, receives. Everyone who seeks, finds. And to everyone who knocks, the door will be opened.

"You parents—if your children ask for a loaf of bread, do you give them a stone instead? Or if they ask for a fish, do you give them a snake? Of course not! So if you sinful people know how to give good gifts to your children, how much more will your heavenly Father give good gifts to those who ask him.

The Golden Rule

"Do to others whatever you would like them to do to you. This is the essence of all that is taught in the law and the prophets.

The Narrow Gate

"You can enter God's Kingdom only through the narrow gate. The highway to hell is broad, and its gate is wide for the many who choose that way. But the gateway to life is very narrow and the road is difficult, and only a few ever find it.

The Tree and Its Fruit

"Beware of false prophets who come disguised as harmless sheep but are really vicious wolves. You can identify them by their fruit, that is, by the way they act. Can you pick grapes from thornbushes, or figs from thistles? A good tree produces good fruit, and a bad tree produces bad fruit. A good tree can't produce bad fruit, and a bad tree can't produce good fruit. So every tree that does not produce good fruit is chopped down and thrown into the fire. Yes, just as you can identify a tree by its fruit, so you can identify people by their actions.

True Disciples

"Not everyone who calls out to me, 'Lord! Lord!' will enter the Kingdom of Heaven. Only those who actually do the will of my Father in heaven will enter. On judgment day many will say to me, 'Lord! Lord! We prophesied in your name and cast out demons in your name and performed many miracles in your name.' But I will reply, 'I never knew you. Get away from me, you who break God's laws.'

Building on a Solid Foundation"Anyone who listens to my teaching and follows it is wise, like a person who builds a house on solid rock. Though the rain comes in torrents and the floodwaters rise and the winds beat against that house, it won't collapse because it is built on bedrock. But anyone who hears my teaching and doesn't obey it is foolish, like a person who builds a house on sand. When the rains and floods come and the winds beat against that house, it will collapse with a mighty crash."

When Jesus had finished saying these things the crowds were amazed at his teaching, for he taught with real authority—quite unlike their teachers of religious law.

APPENDIX TWO

The Ten Commandments
Exodus 20:2–17

"I am the LORD your God, who rescued you from the land of Egypt, the place of your slavery.

"You must not have any other god but me.

"You must not make for yourself an idol of any kind or an image of anything in the heavens or on the earth or in the sea. You must not bow down to them or worship them, for I, the LORD your God, am a jealous God who will not tolerate your affection for any other gods. I lay the sins of the parents upon their children; the entire family is affected—even children in the third and fourth generations of those who reject me. But I lavish unfailing love for a thousand generations on those who love me and obey my commands.

"You must not misuse the name of the LORD your God. The LORD will not let you go unpunished if you misuse his name.

"Remember to observe the Sabbath day by keeping it holy. You have six days each week for your ordinary work, but the seventh day is a Sabbath day of rest dedicated to the Lord your God. On that day no one in your household may do any work. This includes you, your sons and daughters, your male and female servants, your livestock, and any foreigners living among you. For in six days the Lord made the heavens, the earth, the sea, and everything in them; but on the seventh day he rested. That is why the Lord blessed the Sabbath day and set it apart as holy.

"Honor your father and mother. Then you will live a long, full life in the land the Lord your God is giving you.

"You must not murder.

"You must not commit adultery.

"You must not steal.

"You must not testify falsely against your neighbor.

"You must not covet your neighbor's house. You must not covet your neighbor's wife, male or female servant, ox or donkey, or anything else that belongs to your neighbor."

APPENDIX THREE

John 9:1, 6–34

As Jesus was walking along, he saw a man who had been blind since birth. . . .

Then he spit on the ground, made mud with the saliva, and spread the mud over the blind man's eyes. He told him, "Go wash yourself in the pool of Siloam" . . . So the man went and washed and came back seeing!

His neighbors and others who knew him as a blind beggar asked each other, "Isn't this the man who used to sit and beg?" Some said he was, and others said, "No, he just looks like him!"

But the beggar kept saying, "Yes, I am the same one!"

They asked, "Who healed you? What happened?"

He told them, "The man they call Jesus made mud and spread it over my eyes and told me, 'Go to the pool of Siloam and wash yourself.' So I went and washed and now I can see!"

"Where is he now?" they asked.

"I don't know," he replied.

Then they took the man who had been blind to the Pharisees, because it was on the Sabbath that Jesus had made the mud and healed him. The Pharisees asked the man all about it. So he told them, "He put the mud over my eyes, and when I washed it away, I could see!"

Some of the Pharisees said, "This man Jesus is not from God, for he is working on the Sabbath." Others said, "But how could an ordinary sinner do such miraculous signs?" So there was deep division of opinion among them.

Then the Pharisees again questioned the man who had been blind and demanded, "What's your opinion about this man who healed you?"

The man replied, "I think he must be a prophet."

The Jewish leaders still refused to believe the man had been blind and could now see, so they called in his parents. They asked them, "Is this your son? Was he born blind? If so, how can he now see?"

His parents replied, "We know this is our son and that he was born blind, but we don't know how he can see or who healed him. Ask him. He is old enough to speak for himself." His parents said this because they were afraid of the Jewish leaders, who had announced that anyone saying Jesus was the Messiah would be expelled from the synagogue. That's why they said, "He is old enough. Ask him."

So for the second time they called in the man who had been blind and told him, "God should get the glory for this, because we know this man Jesus is a sinner."

"I don't know whether he is a sinner," the man replied. "But I know this: I was blind, and now I can see!"

"But what did he do?" they asked, "How did he heal you?"

"Look!" the man exclaimed. "I told you once. Didn't you listen? Why do you want to hear it again? Do you want to become his disciples, too?"

Then they cursed him and said, "You are his disciple, but we are disciples of Moses! We know God spoke to Moses, but we don't even know where this man comes from."

"Why, that's very strange!" the man replied. "He healed my eyes, and yet you don't know where he comes from? We know that God doesn't listen to sinners, but he is ready to hear those who worship him and do his will. Ever since the world began, no one has been able to open the eyes of someone born blind. If this man were not from God, he couldn't have done it."

"You were born a total sinner!" they answered. "Are you trying to teach us?" And they threw him out of the synagogue.

APPENDIX FOUR

Romans 7:14–8:4
Struggling with Sin

So the trouble is not with the law, for it is spiritual and good. The trouble is with me, for I am all too human, a slave to sin. I don't really understand myself, for I want to do what is right, but I don't do it. Instead, I do what I hate. But if I know that what I am doing is wrong, this shows that I agree that the law is good. So I am not the one doing wrong; it is sin living in me that does it.

And I know that nothing good lives in me, that is, in my sinful nature. I want to do what is right, but I can't. I want to do what is good, but I don't. I don't want to do what is wrong, but I do it anyway. But if I do what I don't want to do, I am not really the one doing wrong; it is sin living in me that does it.

I have discovered this principle of life—that when I want to do what is right, I inevitably do what is wrong. I love God's law with all my heart. But there is another power within me that is at war with my mind. This power makes me a slave to the sin that is still within me. Oh, what a miserable person I am! Who will free me from this life that is dominated by sin and death? Thank God! The answer is in Jesus Christ our Lord. So you see how it is: In my mind I really want to obey God's law, but because of my sinful nature I am a slave to sin.

Life in the Spirit

So now there is no condemnation for those who belong to Christ Jesus. And because you belong to him, the power of the life-giving Spirit has freed you from the power of sin that leads to death. The law of Moses was unable to save us because of the weakness of our sinful nature. So God did what the law could not do. He sent his own Son in a body like the bodies we sinners have. And in that body God declared an end to sin's control over us by giving his Son as a sacrifice for our sins. He did this so that the just requirement of the law would be fully satisfied for us, who no longer follow our sinful nature but instead follow the Spirit.

APPENDIX FIVE

12 Steps = The Christian Walk

Step 1—*We admitted we were powerless over our addictions and compulsive behaviors, that our lives had become unmanageable*—is an invitation to face reality and admit that our life isn't working with us in control. We stop pretending that it IS working, we admit our powerlessness, and we stop trying to manage our life OUR way. The idea that there are areas of our lives over which we are powerless may be a new idea to some and a difficult one to embrace. It is much easier and more comfortable to believe that we are in control of ourselves and our lives. Healing, however, begins when we admit our problems.

The idea of taking this first step can be overwhelming until we stop looking at our lives through the lens of DENIAL and start seeing them through the lens of reality.

We may have been taught to believe that we only have to accept Christ as our Lord and Savior for our lives to be complete and satisfying. Our proclamation that "I am a born again Christian; my past is washed clean; I am a new creature; Christ has totally changed me" is true. Our Spirits are born again. Our flesh, however, is holding on to a lifetime of hurts, habits and hang-ups. We need more than salvation. We need transformation. We need change. To overspiritualize the initial work of salvation may be to deny the actual condition of our lives.

Step 1, if worked properly, leaves us feeling empty and ready for Step 2— *We came to believe that a power greater than ourselves could restore us to sanity.* When we begin to see that help is available to us and as we reach out and accept what our Higher Power has to offer, we start to feel hopeful that our life will improve and we'll feel better. To take this step we need not understand what lies ahead. We need to trust that God knows what lies ahead and that He loves us and will take care of us.

Taking Step 2 positions us to take Step 3—*We made a decision to turn our lives and our wills over to the care of God.* In the first 2 steps we became aware of our condition and accepted the idea of a power greater than ourselves. Step 3 is decision time. When we take Step 3 God becomes the manager of our life and we learn to accept life on His terms. Many of us initially take Step 3 by turning over only certain parts of our lives to God. We are willing to turn over the problematic parts of our lives when we see they are making our lives unmanageable; however, we hold onto other parts of our lives thinking we can manage them just fine, thank you very much. We eventually realize, however, that we cannot barter with God. We must surrender our entire will and every area of our life to His care if we really want to recover. When we are finally able and willing to accept this reality, our journey to wholeness begins for real and we are ready to work Step 4.

Step 4—*We made a searching and fearless moral inventory of ourselves*—opens our eyes to the weaknesses in our lives that need changing and helps us to build on our strengths. We examine our behavior and expand our understanding of ourselves. As we begin to see ourselves clearly, we learn to accept our whole character—the good and the bad. As our self-discovery unfolds, we begin to recognize the role that denial has played in our lives. This realization is the basis for embracing the truth of our personal history. An honest and thorough inventory leads to self-acceptance and freedom.

Step 5—*We admitted to God, to ourselves and to another human being the exact nature of our wrongs*—gives us the opportunity to set aside our pride as we see ourselves through the lens of reality. Step 5 is a pathway out of isolation and loneliness and results in freedom, happiness and serenity. Working Step 5 lays a new foundation for our life of relationship to God and commitment to honesty and humility. Our growing relationship with God gives us the courage to examine ourselves and reveal our true self to ourselves, to God and to another human being. Self-disclosure is an important part of our Christian walk. We were created to live in community with both God and people. Authentic community requires disclosure. It is tempting to believe that telling God is all that is necessary because He ultimately forgives all sins. While this is true, confession to another human being provides special healing and wholeness and releases the grip of hidden sin. Once we share our inventory with God and with another human being we are ready to move on to Step 6.

Step 6—*We were entirely ready to have God remove all these defects of character*—provides us with a needed rest as God works in us to create needed change. Our task in this step is to develop the willingness to respond to God's desired action in our lives. We may believe the saying "God helps those who help themselves, so get busy and change." This, however, is not true. Change comes from God, not from our self-will, and it comes when we are willing to Let Go and Let God!

In Step 7—*We humbly ask Him to remove all our shortcomings*—we Let God. We work this step on our knees in humble prayer, asking God to remove our shortcomings, one defect at a time. Asking God to remove our defects is a true measure of our willingness to surrender control. For those of us who have spent our lives thinking we were self-sufficient, surrendering control can be an extremely difficult task. It is also an extremely freeing task. It takes much faith and trust to work this step. We need to remember that God hears us and wants to answer our prayer. We also need to remember that God works on *His* timetable, not ours. He will remove our defects when He knows we are ready.

Step 8—*Made a list of all persons we had harmed, and became willing to make amends to them all*—begins the process of healing damaged relationships. Up to this point in our recovery we have been looking at and dealing with how our hurts, habits and hang-ups have affected us. We now begin to look at how they have harmed others. Reviewing our Fourth Step inventory helps us determine who belongs on our list. Once our amends list is done we are ready to move on to Step 9—*We made direct amends to such people whenever possible, except when to do so would injure them or others.* This step gives us the opportunity to take concrete action to heal the damage of our past and to move further along on the pathway out of isolation and loneliness. Accepting responsibility for the harm we've done to others is a humbling experience because it forces us to admit the effect we have had on people that we care about. It requires much courage to successfully complete this step. It is not easy to admit to someone face to face that we have hurt him or her and to ask for forgiveness. Doing this, however, leads to increased self-esteem, serenity, and peace, both in ourselves and in our relationships.

Steps 8 & 9 help us repair our past. Step 10—*We continued to take personal inventory and when we were wrong promptly admitted it*—is a maintenance step that is designed to help us stay on track in our recovery. Doing a daily inventory and making amends as needed strengthens and protects our recovery and is a vital part of walking a healthy Christian walk.

Step 11—*We sought through prayer and meditation to improve our conscious contact with God, praying only for knowledge of His will for us and power to carry that out*—is another maintenance step. Our relationship with God is our most important relationship. In order for that relationship to be vibrant and alive, ongoing honest communication is critical. As we draw near to God in prayer and meditation, we draw close to our source of power, serenity, guidance and healing. To ignore communication with God is to unplug our power source.

Step 12—*Having had a spiritual experience as the result of these steps, we try to carry this message to others and to practice these principles in all our affairs*—is an action step. Step 12 calls us to reach out to those who are hurting and struggling, and to share with them our experience, strength and hope. First Peter 3:10 tells us: "Always be prepared to give an answer to everyone who asks you to give the reason for the hope that you have." The most powerful way that we can work Step 12 of carrying this message to others is to actually WALK the Christian walk, to walk the walk, not just talk the talk. When working Step 12 a good rule of thumb is "Actions speak louder than words." There is no more powerful witness of God's transformational love and power than a transformed life that lives that transformation day in and day out.

NOTES

1   Margery Williams Bianco, *The Velveteen Rabbit* (Kennebunkport, Maine: Cider Mill Press Book Publishers 2012) 10–11.

2   Hans Christian Andersen., www.online-literature. com/hans_christian_andersen/981/

3   Rick Warren, *The Purpose Driven Life* (Grand Rapids, Michigan: Zondervan, 2002) 191.

4   Sharon Wegscheider, *Another Chance: Hope and Health for the Alcoholic Family* (Palo Alto, CA: Science and Behavior Books, Inc. 1981) 104.

5   Ibid., 107–108

6   Michael Elkin, *Families under the Influence: Changing Alcoholic Patterns* (Don Mills, Ontario, Canada: Stoddart, a subsidiary of General Publishing Co. Ltd., 1984) 60

7   Ibid.

8   Margaret Fiero, *When Caretaking Becomes an Unhealthy Equilibrium*, just mind blog, November 11, 2014.

9   John Bradshaw, *Healing The Shame That Binds You* (Deerfield Beach, Florida: Health Communications, Inc., 1988) 10.

10 Charles M. Whitfield, MD, *Healing The Child Within* (Deerfield Beach, Florida: Health Communications, Inc., 1987) 43–45.

11 Alan D. Wright, *Shame Off You* (Sisters, Oregon: Multnomah Publishers, Inc., 2005) 28.

12 Charles M. Whitfield, MD, *Healing The Child Within* (Deerfield Beach, Florida: Health Communications, Inc., 1987) 46

13 Alan D. Wright, *Shame Off You* (Sisters, Oregon: Multnomah Publishers, Inc., 2005) 96–98.

14 John Bradshaw, *Healing The Shame That Binds You* (Deerfield Beach, Florida: Health Communications, Inc., 1988) 7.

15 Ibid., 10–14.

16 Alan D. Wright, *Shame Off You* (Sisters, Oregon: Multnomah Publishers, Inc., 2005) 31-33.

17 James G. McCarthy, *The Gospel According to Rome* (Eugene, Oregon: Harvest House Publishers, 1995) 84.

18 Ibid., 85–86.

19 Ibid., 63.

20 Ibid., 55–56.

21 Ibid., 57 .

22 Ibid., 63–65.

23 Bruxy Cavey, *The End of Religion* (Colorado Springs, Colorado: NavPress, 2007) 37.

24 Richard Byrd Wilke and Julia Kitchens Wilke, *Disciple: Becoming Disciples Through Bible Study, Study Manual* (Abingdon Press, 1993) 103–104.

25 John Fischer, *12 Steps for the Recovering Pharisee (Like Me)* (Minneapolis, Minnesota: Bethany House Publishers, 2000) 10.

26 George Weinberg, *The Heart of Psychotherapy* (New York, New Yok: St. Martin's Press, 1984) 9.

27 Donald B. Kraybill, Steven M. Nolt and David L. Weaver-Zercher, *Amish Grace; How Forgiveness Transcended Tragedy* (San Francisco, California: Jossey-Bass, 2007) 49.

28 Ibid., 47.

29 John Bradshaw, *Healing the Shame That Binds You* (Deerfield Beach, Florida: Health Communications, Inc., 1988) 121.

30 Rick Warren, *The Purpose Driven Life* (Grand Rapids, Michigan: Zondervan, 2002) 234.

31 Bill Hybels, *Too Busy Not to Pray* (Downers Grove, Illinois: InterVarsity Press, 1998) 148.

32 Ibid., 179

33 Rick Warren, *The Purpose Driven Life* (Grand Rapids, Michigan: Zondervan, 2002) 64.

34 Rick Muchow, *The Worship Answer Book* (Nashville, Tennessee: J. Countryman, a division of Thomas Nelson, Inc., 2006) 7.

35 Joyce Meyer, *The Power of Simple Prayer* (New York, New York: FaithWords Hachette Book Group USA, 2007) 92.

36 Ibid., 94.

37 Bill Hybels, *Courageous Leadership* (Grand Rapids, Michigan: Zondervan, 2002) 15.

38 Ibid., 23.

39 Joyce Meyer, *Religion or Relationship* CD, (Fenton, Missouri: Joyce Meyer Ministries).

40   Henry and Richard Blackaby, *Spiritual Leadership* (Nashville, Tennessee: Broadman & Holman Publishers, 2001) 46.

41   Ibid., 36–.37

42   Ibid., 43.

43   Ibid., 21.

44   Ibid., 22.

45   Ibid., 75–76.

46   John C. Maxwell, *The Maxwell Leadership Bible* (Nashville, Tennessee: Thomas Nelson, 2002) 212.

47   Ibid., 106.

48   Joyce Meyer, *A Leader in the Making* (New York, New York: Warner Books, 2001) 141.

49   Bill Hybels, *Courageous Leadership* (Grand Rapids, Michigan: Zondervan, 2002) 31–35.

50   Bruxy Cavey, *The End of Religion* (Colorado Springs, Colorado: NavPress, 2007) 212–213.

51   Marcus J. Borg, *Jesus A New Vision* (San Francisco, California: Harper & Row, 1987) 192–193.

52   Gregory A Boyd, *Repenting of Religion* (Grand Rapids, Michigan: BakerBooks, 2004) 54.

53   Bruxy Cavey, *The End of Religion* (Colorado Springs, Colorado: NavPress, 2007) 116–117.

54   Ibid., 82.

55   Rick Warren, *The Purpose Driven Life* (Grand Rapids, Michigan: Zondervan, 2002) 234–235.

56   John C. Maxwell, *Becoming a Person of Influence* (Siloam Springs, Arkansas: Gaborgs, a division of DaySpring Cards, Inc., 2003).

57 Bill Hybels, *Too Busy Not to Pray* (Downers Grove, Illinois: InterVarsity Press, 1998) 125.

58 Henry and Richard Blackaby, *Spiritual Leadership* (Nashville, Tennessee: Broadman & Holman Publishers, 2001) 62.

59 Bruxy Cavey, *The End of Religion* (Colorado Springs, Colorado: NavPress, 2007) 213.

60 Gregory A. Boyd, *Repenting of Religion* (Grand Rapids, Michigan: BakerBooks, 2004) 45.

61 Ibid., 181.

62 Bill Hybels, *Courageous Leadership* (Grand Rapids, Michigan: Zondervan, 2002) 18–21.

63 Neil T. Anderson, Rich Miller and Paul Travis, *Breaking the Bondage of Legalism* (Eugene, Oregon: Harvest House Publishers, 2003) 37.

64 Bruxy Cavey, *The End of Religion* (Colorado Springs, Colorado: NavPress, 2007) 65.

65 Bill Hybels, *Courageous Leadership* (Grand Rapids, Michigan: Zondervan, 2002) 22.

66 Bruxy Cavey, *The End of Religion* (Colorado Springs, Colorado: NavPress, 2007) 222–223.

67 Bill Hybels, *Too Busy Not to Pray* (Downers Grove, Illinois: InterVarsity Press, 1998) 164.

68 Lewis B. Smedes, *The Art of Forgiving; When You Need to Forgive and Don't Know How* (New York, New York: The Random House Publishing Group, 1996) xii-xiii.

69 Lewis B. Smedes, *Forgive & Forget; Healing the Hurts We Don't Deserve* (New York, New York: HarperCollins Publishers, 1984) 94.

70 Rick Warren, *The Purpose Driven Life* (Grand Rapids, Michigan: Zondervan, 2002) 241.

71 *The Life Recovery Bible* (Carol Stream, Illinois: Tyndale House Publishers, 1998) 1401.